K Fletcher

THINKING SKILLS

DAILY BRAIN TEASERS

AGES 5–7

GEORGIE BEASLEY

CREDITS

Author
Georgie Beasley

Illustrations
Nick Diggory

Editor
Kim Vernon

Series Designer
Anna Oliwa

Assistant Editor
Margaret Eaton

Designer
Melissa Leeke

Text © Georgie Beasley
© 2006 Scholastic Ltd

Designed using Adobe InDesign

Published by Scholastic Ltd
Villiers House, Clarendon Avenue,
Leamington Spa, Warwickshire CV32 5PR

www.scholastic.co.uk

Printed by Bell and Bain Ltd

3 4 5 6 7 8 9   6 7 8 9 0 1 2 3 4 5

British Library Cataloguing-in-Publication Data
A catalogue record for this book is available from the
British Library.

ISBN 0-439-96542-X
ISBN 978-0439-96542-2

The right of Georgie Beasley to be identified as the author
of this work has been asserted by her in accordance with
the Copyright, Designs and Patents Act 1988.

Material from the National Curriculum © The Queen's
Printer and Controller of HMSO. Reproduced under the
terms of HMSO Guidance Note 8.

CONTENTS

DAILY BRAINTEASERS FOR AGES 5–7

WHAT IS *DAILY BRAINTEASERS*?

Daily Brainteasers 5–7 is a collection of over 160 ideas for activities that will develop the five thinking skills highlighted in the National Curriculum.

HOW IS IT ORGANISED?

Different children prefer different learning styles: visual (seeing), auditory (hearing), tactile (touching); kinaesthetic (movement). The activities have been grouped into four chapters, each focusing on one of the learning styles.

WHAT DOES EACH BRAINTEASER CONTAIN?

● Each brainteaser details the thinking skill to be developed:

Information processing – collecting, sorting, classifying, sequencing, comparing and contrasting information.

Reasoning – giving reasons for opinions and actions, drawing inferences, making deductions, using precise language to convey ideas, making judgements and decisions based on reason/evidence.

Enquiry – asking relevant questions, posing and defining problems, planning what to do and how to research, predicting outcomes and anticipating consequences, testing conclusions and improving ideas.

Creative – generating and extending ideas, suggesting hypotheses, applying imagination, looking for alternative, innovative outcomes.

Evaluation – evaluating information, judging the value of what is read, seen, heard or done, developing criteria for judging the value of their own and others' work or ideas, and developing confidence in their judgements.

(adapted from National Curriculum, 2000)

● Each brainteaser states if there is a link to another learning style.

● It details the subject link – many of the brainteasers are activities that complement objectives in the units from the Year 1 and Year 2 QCA schemes of work.

● Each brainteaser gives suggestions for organisation. Many of the ideas are flexible and can be adapted for teachers' individual situations.

● A list of resources is given and some refer to useful websites (live at the time of publication).

● Instructions for carrying out the brainteasers are given in the WHAT TO DO section. Where possible these have been directed at the children themselves.

● Answers to problems have also been given where appropriate!

HOW SHOULD THEY BE USED?

Daily Brainteasers is designed to provide ideas for short purposeful ten-minute activities that challenge the children's thinking and cater for the range of learning styles. Many can be led by any adult working in the classroom. Some can be given to the children themselves for self-directed learning. Other brainteasers provide starting points for more concentrated activities, while a few provide useful assessments before introducing or after completing a unit of work.

The purpose of these short tasks is to introduce the main thinking challenge(s) outlined above and which should take up the bulk of the time. There is no need to follow up the activities in detail because additional short brainteasers will emerge naturally, the activity will be completed in the short time available or learning will be followed up in longer lessons later in the day or week.

COLOUR MAGIC

THINKING SKILL: creative thinking
SUBJECT LINK: art and design, science
LEARNING LINK: auditory
ORGANISATION: small groups or pairs
RESOURCES: colour charts available from DIY stores; scissors, glue, pencils and a sheet of paper for each group

WHAT TO DO

● Look at a colour chart and read the names of the colours. Choose the ones that you like.
● Do the colour names match the colours?
● Choose another colour chart and this time, ask your friends to close their eyes.
● Choose a colour and say its name.
● Ask your friends to open their eyes and guess the colour from its name.
● Let your friends have a turn so that you can guess the colour.

NOW TRY THIS

1. Cut out three squares of colour from the colour chart. Do not cut out the colour names.
2. Stick the colours to a sheet of paper.
3. Talk together about each colour and make up some names for each one.
4. Choose one name for each colour.
5. List the names underneath.
6. Get together with another group. Guess each other's colours from the names you have given them.

COLOUR ORDER

THINKING SKILL: information processing
SUBJECT LINK: art and design, science, ICT
LEARNING LINK: kinaesthetic
ORGANISATION: small groups
RESOURCES: colours cut out from colour charts; glue; a long sheet of paper for each group; paints, brushes, mixing palettes and water

WHAT TO DO

● Collect a pile of colours. Spread them out in the middle of your table.
● Sort them into sets of the same colour.
● For each colour set, line them in a strip from the palest to the darkest.
● By the side of each strip, write down which colours you think were mixed to make the tones and tints.

NOW TRY THIS

1. Choose one strip of colour each and try to make the colours by using your list.
2. Mix and match each colour.
3. Use a computer program such as *Dazzle* to find the tints and tones. Recreate your colour strips on screen.
4. Save the colours to a file or print them.

A CIRCLE OF SHAPES

THINKING SKILL: reasoning
SUBJECT LINK: mathematics
LEARNING LINK: kinaesthetic, tactile
ORGANISATION: small group
RESOURCES: sets of Logiblocs™ or similar

WHAT TO DO

● Look at the shapes. Sort them first by colour, then by size, then by shape and then by thickness.
● Make a row of thick shapes and a row of thin shapes.
● Make a row of circles, triangles, squares and rectangles.
● Make a row of big shapes and a row of small shapes.

● Make a row of yellow shapes, red shapes and blue shapes.

NOW TRY THIS

1. Play this game with the blocks, as if you were playing dominoes. Put one shape in the middle of the table. Next to it place a shape that is the same in only one way (perhaps same colour or thickness).
2. Continue to add shapes in this way, keeping one thing the same each time, until you cannot put any more shapes in the line. How many shapes have you got?
3. Play the game again. Try to make your line longer.
4. Make a circle of shapes around the edge of your table.

SPELLING MISTAKES

THINKING SKILL: evaluation
SUBJECT LINK: English (literacy), ICT
LEARNING LINK: auditory, kinaesthetic
ORGANISATION: individuals or pairs
RESOURCES: lists of spellings, some correct and some not (use spellings the children have recently learned or take them from the high frequency lists for the year); highlighter pens and red crayons; sheets of paper; pencils

WHAT TO DO

● Look at each word in your list.
● Decide with a friend which ones are spelled correctly.
● Highlight those that you think are not and underline them with a squiggly red line, like the computer does.
● Ask an adult to check you have highlighted the correct words or check them against the classroom charts.
● Write the words correctly by the side.

NOW TRY THIS

1. Spell each of the words out loud.
2. After spelling out loud, cover up the word and try to write it out correctly on a separate piece of paper.
3. Now try to spell the words from memory, taking it in turns to read them first.

SPOT THE DIFFERENCE

THINKING SKILL: enquiry, information processing
SUBJECT LINK: art and design, mathematics
LEARNING LINK: kinaesthetic
ORGANISATION: whole class, pairs
RESOURCES: a set of 3-D shapes; a digital camera; two photographs taken of the same 3-D shapes, one photograph showing the shapes in different positions and with two additional shapes to the first set; print enough photographs for each pair or display on a whiteboard/OHP

WHAT TO DO

● Look at the photographs on your table.
● Talk to a friend about how they are different.
● Agree the differences with the rest of the class.

NOW TRY THIS

1. Choose one of the photographs.
2. Find and arrange the 3-D shapes to match the photograph. Take a photo, print it out and compare your photo with the first one.
3. Put a ring round the differences.

ALL GROUPS TOGETHER

THINKING SKILL: information processing
SUBJECT LINK: science
LEARNING LINK: kinaesthetic, auditory
ORGANISATION: whole class and small groups
RESOURCES: a range of objects and packaging that can be classified into groups, such as fruits, vegetables, sugary foods, dairy, meat, wheat, fish

WHAT TO DO

● Look at the things in your collection. Organise them into sets according to groups by the type of food they are.
● Talk to each other to help you do this.
● You can have up to seven groups: fish, meat, wheat products, dairy, sugary foods, vegetables and fruits.

NOW TRY THIS

1. Sort the whole collection as a class so that each food group is placed on its own table.
2. Find out:
   a. Which table has the most/least sugar?
   b. Which table has the most/least fat?
3. Decide which are the healthiest foods and which are not healthy.

FAMILY GROUPS

THINKING SKILL: reasoning
SUBJECT LINK: mathematics
LEARNING LINK: tactile
ORGANISATION: small groups
RESOURCES: several packs of 'Happy Family' cards or use photographs of actual families (be sensitive to one-parent families); large sheets of paper divided into Carroll diagrams

WHAT TO DO

● Look at the people on your cards. Sort them into families.

● Place your cards in rows and columns so that they are in family groups and the same family members are in the same columns.

● Go around the groups to see if your groupings are the same.

NOW TRY THIS

1. Write labels and use Carroll diagrams to sort your 'Happy Families' – for example, 'baker', 'not baker', 'Mrs', 'not Mrs'.

2. Swap with another group and complete each other's challenges. Write different labels for other groups to try.

3. Use Logiblocs™ or sort teddies. Organise these by using Carroll diagrams.

4. Use this method of sorting to identify with a friend the shapes that are round and not yellow, those that are thick and red, and so on.

THE THREE LITTLE PIGS

THINKING SKILL: reasoning
SUBJECT LINK: English (literacy)
LEARNING LINK: kinaesthetic
ORGANISATION: groups of three
RESOURCES: pictures or actual objects of: three identical pigs; a red, a blue and a yellow scarf; a straw house, stick house and brick house; a toy car, toy aeroplane, teddy bear

WHAT TO DO

● The Three Little Pigs have favourite scarves and toys.

● Read the following clues. Work out which little pig wears which scarf.

> **Clue 1** The little pig who lives in the straw house does not wear the red scarf.
>
> **Clue 2** The little pig who wears the blue scarf does not live in the brick house.
>
> **Clue 3** The little pig who lives in the stick house wears the yellow scarf.

● Match the scarves to the correct little pig and put him by the house.

NOW TRY THIS

Work out which toy is each little pig's favourite.

> **Clue 1** The little pig who wears the yellow scarf does not like the toy car.
>
> **Clue 2** The little pig who lives in the house of straw does not like the teddy bear.
>
> **Clue 3** The little pig who wears the red scarf likes the teddy bear.

ANSWERS

	Straw	Sticks	Brick
Red	X	X	YES
Blue	YES	X	X
Yellow	X	YES	X

	Car	Aeroplane	Teddy bear
Yellow sticks	X	YES	X
Red brick	X	X	YES
Blue straw	YES	X	X

SNAP AT EVERY TURN

THINKING SKILL: information processing, reasoning
SUBJECT LINK: mathematics
LEARNING LINK: tactile
ORGANISATION: pairs
RESOURCES: sets of pictures or cards suitable for playing Snap (one per pair)

WHAT TO DO

● Play Snap with a partner until you are familiar with the pictures.

NOW TRY THIS

1. Join with another pair of children. Organise the cards in both packs in the same order so that every time you turn a card you can say *Snap*.
2. Play the game to see if you have succeeded.
3. Shuffle the cards and sort them into a different order.
4. Play Snap to see if you are right again.

CAPITAL LETTERS

THINKING SKILL: information processing
SUBJECT LINK: English (literacy)
LEARNING LINK: kinaesthetic
ORGANISATION: individuals or pairs
RESOURCES: local newspapers; children's magazines; photocopied extracts from a book (subject to your CLA Licence); highlighter pens

WHAT TO DO

● Choose a newspaper or magazine. Use a highlighter to mark all the capital letters you can find on one page.
● Look at the capital letters and decide whether:
  1. They start a new sentence.
  2. It is the word 'I'.
  3. It is a name for something, someone or somewhere.

NOW TRY THIS

Using another example of text, highlight the capital letters that start a sentence in one colour, those that show a name in another and the 'I' words in another.

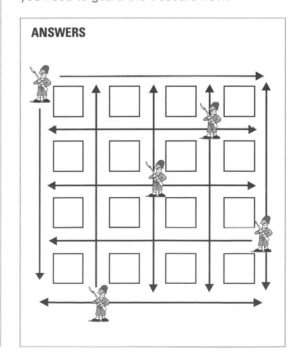

GUARDING THE TREASURE

THINKING SKILL: reasoning
SUBJECT LINK: mathematics
LEARNING LINK: kinaesthetic
ORGANISATION: small groups
RESOURCES: 4x4 and 5x5 grids (see answers below for layout); small-world people and treasure (or people and treasure drawn on small circles that fit inside the grid squares)

WHAT TO DO

● Place the treasure anywhere on the 4x4 grid.
● Decide where you would put the people to guard the treasure. They can see along each of the rows and columns.
● What is the least number of people you need to guard the treasure?

NOW TRY THIS

1. Put the treasure in a different place on the grid.
2. How many people do you need now?
3. Use the 5x5 grid and see how many people you need to guard the treasure now.

ANSWERS

VISUAL LEARNING

REFLECTIONS

THINKING SKILL: enquiry
SUBJECT LINK: art and design
LEARNING LINK: auditory
ORGANISATION: small groups or whole class
RESOURCES: mirrors

WHAT TO DO

● Look around the classroom. Note things around you that you usually take for granted like tables, chairs, door, windows and resources.
● Look in the mirror. Identify all these things from their reflections. Do they look the same? Share your opinions with a friend.
● Tilt the mirror away from you, upwards and to both sides.
● Look at the ceiling and through any windows or doors.
● How easy is it to recognise your friends from their reflections?
● Use the mirror to look over your shoulder.
● Did you see what you expected to see?

NOW TRY THIS

1. Go outside onto the playground or school field.
2. Stand still and use the mirror to look all around you.
3. Talk to a friend about what you can see.
4. Decide whether things look different or the same to the way they usually look and if so, how and why.
5. Return to the classroom. Write a list or draw pictures of what you saw in the mirror.

WORDS WITHIN WORDS

THINKING SKILL: information processing
SUBJECT LINK: English (literacy)
ORGANISATION: individuals or pairs
RESOURCES: local newspaper, magazines or photocopied extracts from a book (subject to your CLA Licence); highlighter pens; paper; pencils

WHAT TO DO

● Look at your newspaper, magazine or book extract. Highlight all the smaller words you can see inside bigger words, for example 'cat' in 'caterpillar'.
● When you have found at least ten, try to spell some of the words.
● How does knowing the smaller word inside help you spell much longer words?

NOW TRY THIS

1. Write the word 'together' across the top of your paper.
2. Underneath, write all the smaller words you can see in this word.
3. Do the same for 'outstanding', 'comfortable' and 'important'.

FIND A RAINBOW

THINKING SKILL: information processing
SUBJECT LINK: science
LEARNING LINK: auditory
ORGANISATION: group activity
RESOURCES: a collection of items that do and do not reflect a rainbow, such as CDs, prisms, crystal, mirrors and some shiny metal objects; red, blue and yellow cellophane paper

WHAT TO DO

● Turn the CD into the light and look for reflections. What do you see?
● Sort the objects into two sets – those that reflect different colours and those that do not.
● Look through the prism. Talk about all the colours you can see. Where do you think the colours come from? Which two colours do you think make the colour yellow? Which colours make purple and orange?

NOW TRY THIS

1. Look at objects around the classroom through different-coloured cellophane. What do you notice? Do any appear to change colour?
2. Find a book you can read. Look at the words and pictures through the yellow, red and blue cellophane. Do any make the print look clearer?
3. How many colours can you make by overlapping the cellophanes? Write down your combinations as a sum. For example, red + green = brown.

ANSWER
Explain that the only colours that cannot be mixed are green, blue and red as these are the primary colours of light.

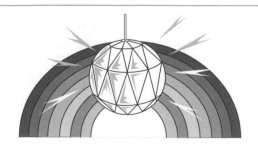

CODES

THINKING SKILL: information processing, reasoning
SUBJECT LINK: English (literacy)
LEARNING LINK: auditory
ORGANISATION: individuals, pairs or small groups
RESOURCES: alphabets found in dictionaries or in the classroom; sheets of paper; pencils

WHAT TO DO

● Say the alphabet through together to remind yourself of the letter order.
● Work out what this joke says:
Xibu ep gspht esjol? Dspblb Dpmb.
● The joke is written in code. The code uses the letter after the one it really is, so A is written as B, B as C and so on.
● Can you work it out now? Use an alphabet line in your classroom or in your dictionary. You could write out the alphabet on paper and underneath write the letter that comes next in the alphabet. This should help to spell out the joke.

Real letter	A	B	C	D	E ...
Code letter	B	C	D	E	F ...

NOW TRY THIS

Turn a favourite (short) joke into your own code for a friend to solve.

> **ANSWER**
> The joke is: What do frogs drink? Croaka Cola.

WORD LADDERS

THINKING SKILL: reasoning, enquiry
SUBJECT LINK: English (literacy)
LEARNING LINK: auditory
ORGANISATION: individuals, pairs or small groups
RESOURCES: sheets of paper; pencils; a two-minute timer

WHAT TO DO

● Write as many three-letter cvc (consonant, vowel, consonant) words as you can in two minutes.
● Choose two words that are very different with none of the same letters, such as dog and pat, cat and rip, pen and dog.
● Write the first word at the top of your paper and underneath change one letter at a time, to make new words, until you have made the second word.

NOW TRY THIS

1. Write as many four-letter words as you can in two minutes.
2. Choose two four-letter words that are very different and change one letter at a time, as a word ladder.

WORD STRANDS

THINKING SKILL: information processing
SUBJECT LINK: English (literacy)
LEARNING LINK: auditory
ORGANISATION: whole-class introduction, small groups
RESOURCES: strips of paper; pencils; word labels for: stream, scream, strain, sprain, splash, switch

WHAT TO DO

● Write the word 'strand' on the board.
● Ask the children to say which letter from this larger word can make a word on its own (a).
● Next ask them to add another letter from 'strand' to make a word with two letters.
● Continue adding one letter at a time to make a new word until you have made the word 'strand', building it up from 'a'.

NOW TRY THIS

1. Look at the words on the labels.
2. Turn them into word strands so that there is a strand of words from one letter to all of the letters to make the final word.
3. Try to make more than one strand for some of the words.

ANSWERS

a	an	and	sand	stand	strand
a	am	Sam	seam	steam	stream
a	am	cam	scam	scram	scream
a	am	ram	ream	cream	scream
a	am	ram	cram	scram	scream
a	an	ran	rain	train	strain
a	an	pan	pain	Spain	sprain
a	as	ash	lash	slash	splash
I	it	wit	with	witch	switch

ORDERING NUMBERS

THINKING SKILL: reasoning
SUBJECT LINK: mathematics
LEARNING LINK: auditory
ORGANISATION: pairs or small groups
RESOURCES: paper; pencils; a one-minute timer; dice

WHAT TO DO

● Write down as many numbers as you can in one minute. Do not write these in order but choose numbers at random between 1 and 50.
● Look at the numbers you have written down.
● Put them in order of size, starting with the smallest and finishing with the largest.

NOW TRY THIS

1. Throw two dice. Make two larger numbers from the two numbers on the dice (for example, if you throw a 5 and 4, you could make 54 and 45). If the two numbers are the same, you can only make one number.
2. Which is the larger number?
3. Which is the smaller? How do you know?
4. Add the two numbers together.
5. Find the difference between the two numbers.
6. Do this at least five times.

ENLARGE A PICTURE

THINKING SKILL: enquiry
SUBJECT LINK: art and design
LEARNING LINK: kinaesthetic
ORGANISATION: individuals
RESOURCES: a simple outline picture like those in colouring books, reduced to A5 and divided into grids; A4 paper with grids twice the size as those on the A5 pictures; pencils

WHAT TO DO

● Look at the picture. What can you see?
● Look at the bottom left-hand square. What is in this square?

● Look at the lines. Where do they start and finish? Do they start halfway down one side, along the top of the square or in the middle?
● Copy what is drawn in this square onto the larger grid. Start your line in exactly the same place on your square as the one you are copying. Move the pencil in exactly the same direction, finishing at exactly the same position on your larger square as the one you are copying.

NOW TRY THIS

1. Move to the next square. Copy what is drawn in this square.
2. Continue until you have copied the drawings in all of the squares onto your A4 grid.
3. Does your picture look like the original?

WHICH FITS WHERE?

THINKING SKILL: information processing
SUBJECT LINK: art and design
LEARNING LINK: tactile
ORGANISATION: small groups
RESOURCES: jigsaw puzzles (with at least 25 pieces) for each group (ask older children to complete about two-thirds of the jigsaws in advance)

WHAT TO DO

● Finish your group's jigsaw (or finish as much as you can in five minutes).
● Go around the tables, looking at each of the jigsaws and noting similarities and differences. Look at the colours, parts of the picture, shape and size of the puzzle pieces.

NOW TRY THIS

1. Take out six pieces of your jigsaw.
2. Ask an adult to swap over some pieces from each jigsaw and put them onto other tables.
3. Close your eyes when they do this.
4. Go round the tables, find your missing pieces and finish your puzzle again.

WHAT WAS THERE?

THINKING SKILL: enquiry
SUBJECT LINK: art and design, geography
LEARNING LINK: auditory
ORGANISATION: pairs
RESOURCES: a photograph of the children at playtime, with the school or other buildings in the background; people cut out from a copy of the same photograph, and displayed on a board; a copy of the picture with different people removed (covered or cut-out, this could be done using a digital camera and a whiteboard)

WHAT TO DO

• Look at the whole photograph together. Talk about the buildings and people you can see.
• With a friend, choose one or two people and imagine what they might be doing. What might they be saying to each other or thinking?
• Look at the people displayed on the board.
• Try to spot these people in the picture.

NOW TRY THIS

1. Look at the other copy of the picture with different characters removed.
2. Without looking at the original, see if you can guess which person is missing from the picture.
3. After two minutes, look at the original and see if you were right.

JOINED UP THINKING

THINKING SKILL: reasoning
SUBJECT LINK: science
LEARNING LINK: tactile
ORGANISATION: small group
RESOURCES: any set of objects taken at random from the classroom (one set per group); a large sheet of paper; pencils

WHAT TO DO

• Look at the objects. Decide which one partners another.
• Put the objects together in pairs according to the way they look, what they are made from or their use.
• Could you pair the objects in a different way? How about in threes or fours?

NOW TRY THIS

1. Place the objects in a circle on a large sheet of paper.
2. Join each object to the next with a line.

3. Write the reason why you have joined these two objects to make a circle of thinking.

WHAT COMES NEXT?

THINKING SKILL: information processing, creative thinking
SUBJECT LINK: mathematics
LEARNING LINK: tactile
ORGANISATION: small groups or pairs
RESOURCES: a range of 2-D shapes

WHAT TO DO

• Choose two shapes and find as many as you can, such as all the circles and squares.
• Make a two-shape repeating pattern so that one shape follows on from the other.

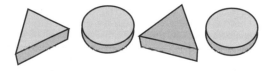

• Swap the shapes around so that you have two of one shape followed by two of another.

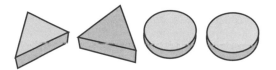

• Start off a repeating pattern for another pair to finish off.

NOW TRY THIS

1. Choose three shapes. Put one shape on top of another. What shapes did you use to make this pattern?
2. Write this down like a sum. The shape at the bottom comes first in the sum, followed by the middle and then the top shape. for example:

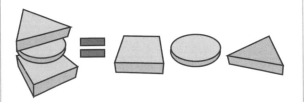

OVER THE WATER

THINKING SKILL: reasoning
SUBJECT LINK: geography
LEARNING LINK: visual, auditory
ORGANISATION: pairs or small groups
RESOURCES: map of a river; pictures or small toys of a boat, hen, fox and bag of corn

WHAT TO DO

● Consider this problem. You need to get the fox, hen and bag of corn from one side of the river to the other using the boat. You can only take one thing across at a time. You cannot leave the fox and hen together as the fox will eat the hen, or the hen and bag of corn together as the hen will eat the corn. How can you get everything across the river?

NOW TRY THIS

Work out how to get a dog, cat and hen across the river. You cannot leave the dog and cat together or the cat and hen. You can only take one animal each time you cross the river.

ANSWERS

First problem – take the hen first leaving the fox and the corn. Go back and fetch the corn. Leave it on the other side and take the hen back. Next pick up the fox and take it over to join the corn. Go back for the hen.

Second challenge – take the cat first. Come back for the hen and leave the hen and bring the cat back. Leave the cat and take the dog. Finally, come back for the cat.

FAMOUS QUESTIONS

THINKING SKILL: enquiry
SUBJECT LINK: history
LEARNING LINK: auditory
ORGANISATION: pairs or small groups
RESOURCES: paper and pencils; some knowledge of the person being researched in history

WHAT TO DO

● Listen to a short story about a famous person you have been learning about in history.
● Tell your friend what you would like to find out about that person.
● Make a list.
● Change your list into questions you would ask that person if you could.
● Write your questions down the left-hand side of another piece of paper.

NOW TRY THIS

1. For each question, identify where and how you could find the answer.
2. Write the possible places on the right-hand side of the paper next to each question.

STRANGE OBJECTS

THINKING SKILL: reasoning
SUBJECT LINK: art and design
LEARNING LINK: auditory
ORGANISATION: individuals or pairs
RESOURCES: photographs of objects in the school grounds or surrounding area, taken from funny angles, or parts of familiar objects taken close up (good objects include flower heads, tree bark, grass, parts of ornate window or door frames, fire bells). Display the photos on a board or whiteboard in two groups, one for the introduction and another harder set for the challenge

WHAT TO DO

● Look at each of the photos in the first set. Talk to a friend about what each could be.
● What are the clues? Think about the colour, shape, features and any information in the background.
● Identify where you would find the object.

NOW TRY THIS

1. Look at the second set of photos. Identify what each one is.
2. Go for a short walk. Identify other interesting objects or parts of objects that would make good photos for this challenge.

SPOT THE OBJECT

THINKING SKILL: information processing
SUBJECT LINK: art and design
LEARNING LINK: auditory
ORGANISATION: pairs
RESOURCES: a simple outline picture divided into grids; a photocopy of the picture cut into squares (give each pair the complete picture and about six of the squares)

WHAT TO DO

● Look at your picture. Talk about what you can see.
● Look at the smaller squares. Where are they in the complete picture?
● Swap over with another group. Where are their smaller squares in the picture?

NOW TRY THIS

1. Look through the pictures from a colouring book.
2. Choose one and make a game. Divide the grids yourself and copy four of the squares. Ask your friends to find which squares you have drawn.

SYMMETRICAL LETTERS

THINKING SKILL: information processing, reasoning
SUBJECT LINK: English (literacy), mathematics
LEARNING LINK: auditory, kinaesthetic
ORGANISATION: individuals or pairs
RESOURCES: a set of capital letters for sorting; a paper set for cutting; scissors

WHAT TO DO

● Identify the letters with a friend. Put them into alphabetical order.
● Divide the set into two smaller subsets of letters that are symmetrical and those that are not.

NOW TRY THIS

1. Take each symmetrical letter, one at a time. Cut it in half along its line of symmetry.
2. Display the two halves side by side.

3. Divide the letters again into those letters that were cut vertically, and those cut horizontally.
4. Which letters could you cut either way?
5. Which letters do you have to turn or rotate to make them fit or show they are symmetrical?
6. Which letter has lots of lines of symmetry?
7. Which letters are not symmetrical?

> **ANSWERS**
> 1. Horizontal lines of symmetry: B, C, D, E, H, I, K.
> 2. Vertical lines of symmetry: A, M, T, U, V, W, Y.
> 3. Horizontal and vertical lines of symmetry: X.
> 4. Letters N, S and Z are only symmetrical if you turn or rotate the two halves.
> 5. F, G, J, L, P, Q, R are not symmetrical.
> 6. The letter O has lots of lines of symmetry because it is round.

ODD ONE OUT

THINKING SKILL: reasoning
SUBJECT LINK: science
LEARNING LINK: auditory
ORGANISATION: whole class, small groups
RESOURCES: pictures as follows:
Set 1: an elderly adult male, an adult female, a male child and a dog
Set 2: a tree, a flower, a bench and an evergreen shrub
Set 3: a plastic toy car, a plastic dice, a teddy and a plastic bowl
Set 4: a butterfly, a frog, a fish and a dragonfly

WHAT TO DO

● Look at the four pictures in Set 1 together as a class.
● Identify each picture and decide which one could be the odd one out.
● Can you give a reason for your decisions?

NOW TRY THIS

1. In groups, look in turn at Sets 2, 3 and 4.
2. Decide which is the odd one out in each set.
3. Choose one set of pictures and stick them on a sheet of paper.
4. Say which is the odd one out, and why.

WHY THIS NAME?

THINKING SKILL: reasoning, creative thinking
SUBJECT LINK: geography
LEARNING LINK: auditory
ORGANISATION: small groups
RESOURCES: a picture of the whole of the Isle of Struay (there is one inside the front cover of *Katie Morag and the New Pier* by Mairi Hedderwick (Red Fox) or in the *Big Katie Morag Storybook*) displayed for all the children to see, or enough books/photocopies for each group (subject to your CLA Licence)

WHAT TO DO

● Look at the map in *Katie Morag and the New Pier* and locate some of the houses and features, such as the stream and mountains, the jetty, beaches, bays, roads and woods.
● Think of answers to these questions:
 1. Why is the New Pier so named?
 2. Why is the jetty called a jetty?
 3. Why is the farm called High Farm?
 4. Who lives in the Holiday House?
 5. Talk about why the Redburn Bridge is so called. What can 'burn' possibly mean? Why is it red?

NOW TRY THIS

1. The mountains are called 'The Five Sisters'. Discuss possible reasons for this name. Can you think of a different name?
2. Create names for the woods, beaches, bays and the new bistro and pier.
3. By the side of your names, give reasons for your decisions.

AT THE POST OFFICE

THINKING SKILL: reasoning
SUBJECT LINK: mathematics
LEARNING LINK: auditory, kinaesthetic
ORGANISATION: individuals or pairs
RESOURCES: a set of 30 stamps for each child or pair (these can be made by hand or using a suitable computer program); scissors; glue; paper

WHAT TO DO

● Mr and Mrs McColl are waiting for a delivery of stamps from the mainland.
● The delivery has not come because the weather is so bad that the boat cannot dock. They only have 1p and 4p stamps left.
● Can their customers send a letter needing 6 pence worth of stamps?
● Can they send a parcel needing 17 pence worth of stamps?
● Is there any price that they cannot make using only 1p and 4p stamps?

NOW TRY THIS

Try the game with only 4p and 2p stamps, 5p and 3p stamps, or 7p and 4p stamps.

KATIE MORAG'S POST OFFICE

THINKING SKILL: enquiry
SUBJECT LINK: English (literacy), geography
LEARNING LINK: auditory
ORGANISATION: pairs or small groups
RESOURCES: photocopies of the inside of Katie Morag's post office from *Katie Morag and the New Pier* by Mairi Hedderwick (Red Fox) for each pair (subject to your CLA Licence); an adult or more able child in each group to read the questions for less able readers

WHAT TO DO

● Look at the picture together. Talk about what you can see – the people, animals and things for sale.
● Look at the notices. What are they saying? Read through the words.

NOW TRY THIS

Answer these questions:
1. Who grew the potatoes?
2. When is the slide show taking place?
3. What is it about?
4. Where is the slide show taking place?
5. How much does the West Highland free press cost?
6. What is its front story about?
7. Who is invited to the AGM of the Struay Show?
8. What sort of party are the islanders collecting for?
9. How many mousetraps are in the box when it is full?

GRANNIE ISLAND

THINKING SKILL: creative thinking
SUBJECT LINK: English (literacy), science, geography
LEARNING LINK: auditory
ORGANISATION: pairs and small groups
RESOURCES: any picture from the Katie Morag stories which shows the route from the post office to Grannie Island's house; a sheet of paper for each group divided into three columns with 'See', 'Hear' and 'Smell' headings

WHAT TO DO

● Look at the picture. Identify as many objects as you can that Katie Morag is likely to see on a walk to see Grannie Island.
● Share what you have found with another group.
● List all of the objects in the first column of your paper.

NOW TRY THIS

1. Look at the picture again. Think of all the things Katie is likely to hear. (Use the list of things she is likely to see as clues.)
2. List these things in the middle column.
3. Have you got as many things she is likely to hear as see?
4. Share them with another pair.
5. Now list all the things that Katie Morag is likely to smell.
6. Have you got as many things she is likely to smell as hear?

KATIE MORAG VISITS GRANNIE MAINLAND

THINKING SKILL: enquiry
SUBJECT LINK: geography
LEARNING LINK: tactile, auditory
ORGANISATION: small groups
RESOURCES: large sheets of paper; pencils; digital camera; scissors (the children will need some knowledge of the Katie Morag stories)

WHAT TO DO

● Talk to the class about what Katie Morag will need to do to prepare for her visit to Grannie Mainland.
● Write these down as sentences on a sheet of paper on separate lines.
● Cut out the things she needs to do. Discuss as a class what she should do first, second and so on. Put the sentences in the right order as the children decide.
● Use a digital camera to record the order.

NOW TRY THIS

1. Look at the sequence. Talk about whether Katie could do things in a different order.
2. Depending on the outcome of your discussions, can you re-order your sequence?
3. Which things can never come first?
4. What will never come last?
5. How many different sequences did you make?

PICTURE FEELINGS

THINKING SKILL: creative thinking
SUBJECT LINK: art and design
LEARNING LINK: auditory
ORGANISATION: small groups
RESOURCES: pictures of different landscapes (motivational)

WHAT TO DO

● Look at a picture together. How does it make you feel?
● Does it make you feel calm, agitated, happy, sad, amused, puzzled or excited?
● Does it make you want to laugh, smile, cry, sleep, run, dance, sing or grin?
● Place the picture in the centre of a large sheet of paper. Write all the words it makes you feel around the outside.

NOW TRY THIS

1. Go to another group. Look at their picture and words. Do you agree? Can you add any other feelings?
2. When you have looked at all of the pictures and added your ideas, go back to your picture and note the words that have been added. Do you agree?

VISUAL LEARNING

MAP KEYS

THINKING SKILL: enquiry
SUBJECT LINK: geography
LEARNING LINK: auditory
ORGANISATION: pairs
RESOURCES: a map of the local area; pencils; small pieces of paper; glue

WHAT TO DO

● Look at the map of the local area with your friend. Identify some of the places.
What natural features can you see?
What features can you see that have been put there by human beings?
What are the buildings and how do you know?
● For each of the natural features, decide on a good picture key to enable someone looking at the map for the first time to identify this. For example, if there is a park with a pond and/or a small wood with trees, you could draw a tree for the wood and a pond for the water.
● Now do the same for the buildings and other features on the map.
● Think about how the map user could identify the different buildings.
● Will you need to make these the same shape on your key as on the map?
● Agree on the symbol for each feature and draw them on a small piece of paper. Think about how to organise them on the paper and about how much space you need to leave between each picture.
● Stick the key to one corner of the map.

THOUGHTFUL BUBBLES

THINKING SKILL: creative thinking
SUBJECT LINK: English (literacy)
LEARNING LINK: auditory
ORGANISATION: small groups or pairs
RESOURCES: picture storybook with familiar characters (one page assigned to each group); cut-out thought bubbles.

WHAT TO DO

● Look at your page in your picture storybook. What is happening? What might the characters be thinking about in this picture?
● Write it down in a thought bubble on your picture.
● Choose one of your group to read the bubble to the class.

● Your teacher will organise the groups in the order of the story.
● In turn, read out the thought bubbles.
● Did your thought bubbles tell a shortened version of the story?

NOW TRY THIS

On your own, look in other storybooks. Find pictures of characters with different looks on their faces. Write thought bubbles on sticky-backed notes and add these to the pictures. Share them with a friend.

KANDINSKY AND FRIENDS

THINKING SKILL: creative thinking
SUBJECT LINK: art and design
LEARNING LINK: kinaesthetic, tactile, auditory
ORGANISATION: small groups
RESOURCES: large space; offcuts of fabric, paper and card; two- and three-dimensional shapes; print of Kandinsky's work such as *Composition VIII*, *Accent en rose*, *Counter-Gravitation*

WHAT TO DO

● Look at a Kandinsky painting. Talk about the shapes, colours and patterns that make up the picture.
● Tell a friend which bits you like and which bits you don't like.
● Listen to what your friend thinks.
● Now talk together as a group. Do you all agree?

NOW TRY THIS

1. Look at the collection of shapes and materials.
2. As a group, choose a space on a table or floor, with a good colour background. Create a picture of your own.
3. This can be like Kandinsky's or can be different.
4. Make a frame from some of the materials.
5. Take a picture.
6. Use paper, card, paint or chalk to recreate your picture during an art lesson, using the photo to remind you of your ideas.

MISFITS

THINKING SKILL: creative thinking
SUBJECT LINK: art and design, English (creative writing)
LEARNING LINK: auditory, kinaesthetic, tactile
ORGANISATION: small groups or pairs
RESOURCES: sheets of paper; pencils

WHAT TO DO

● Without showing anyone else in the group, the first person should draw a person's head at the top of your sheet of paper. Make sure they include a neck.

● Ask them to fold over the paper so that you cannot see the head but you can see the neck.

● The next person draws the body. They should add clothes such as a vest, jumper or T-shirt. Make sure they include the waist before folding the paper over so you cannot see the body but can see the waist.

● The last person draws the legs and then the feet.

● Open up your paper to see the person you have drawn.

● Practise this a few times.

NOW TRY THIS

1. Draw a fantastic animal. You will need to fold the paper in many different ways, depending on where you decide to add the tail and legs.

2. The first person draws the head and then folds this over.

3. The next person draws the body.

4. They should cover over the body with another piece of paper so that the third person can add the legs without seeing the body.

5. Fold over the paper, asking the last person to add a tail.

6. Open up the picture. What fantastic animal have you drawn?

7. Try again. Make your next animal even more fantastic!

8. Choose one of your pictures. Add words to describe your animal's features and a sentence to describe its look. Name your animals.

FAVOURITE CARDS

THINKING SKILL: evaluation
SUBJECT LINK: design and technology
LEARNING LINK: tactile, auditory
ORGANISATION: small groups
RESOURCES: a collection of different types of greetings cards; large sheets of paper; pens

WHAT TO DO

● Choose one of the cards. Talk about what you like and dislike about it.

● Think about the design, colours and greetings message on the front and inside. Does it have any moving parts?

● Agree how many marks out of ten you would give the card. Why?

NOW TRY THIS

1. Repeat this with some of the other cards in the collection.

2. Decide which child in your group will talk about which card to the class. Let them rehearse what they will say. Start by saying how many marks they gave it out of ten and why the group did/did not like it.

PUT YOUR BOOKS IN ORDER

THINKING SKILL: information processing
SUBJECT LINK: English (literacy)
LEARNING LINK: auditory
ORGANISATION: small groups
RESOURCES: a selection of four to six story books, with titles and authors familiar to the children

WHAT TO DO

● Read the title and the name of the author for each book.

● Identify the first letter of the title and the first letter of the author's first name and surname.

● Put the books in alphabetical order according to the title.

● Put the books in alphabetical order according to the author's first name.

● Try it again for the author's surname.

NOW TRY THIS

1. Put them in reverse alphabetical order.

2. Find out if any of the books can be placed in consecutive alphabetical order. This can be done according to the title or the author's name.

VISUAL LEARNING

TWO WORDS INTO ONE

THINKING SKILL: information processing
SUBJECT LINK: English (spelling)
LEARNING LINK: auditory
ORGANISATION: small groups
RESOURCES: a piece of paper; sets of words that can be made into compound words including: black, blue, green, red, bird, berry, board, foot, man, ball, net, snow, straw, cup, super, market, currant, step, house, thorn; highlighters; local newspapers and magazines

WHAT TO DO

● Read the words with a partner.
● Put two words together to make a compound word (a bigger word that can be made by combining two smaller words).
● Write down all the words you can make.
● Now try to pair up all the words to make ten compound words.

NOW TRY THIS

1. Look at a local newspaper or magazine. Highlight all the compound words you can find.
2. Use the words 'any', 'one', 'no', 'some' as your first word and add another word on the end to create as many different compound words as you can.
3. Now use the word 'some' again, but this time use it to add to the end of other words. How many can you find?

MATCHING PHOTOS

THINKING SKILL: information processing
SUBJECT LINK: science
LEARNING LINK: auditory
ORGANISATION: small groups
RESOURCES: photos of children in the group

WHAT TO DO

● Spread out the photos on a table.
● Look at the photos of the children in your group. Talk about the features for about two minutes.
● Each of you should choose a photo by looking, not by touching. Keep the one you have chosen a secret from the rest of the group.
● Take it in turns to give one clue for your group to try to guess the person in the photo you have secretly chosen.
● The person sitting to your right should try to pick out which photo is being described. If she

is right, she should then give a clue to the photo she has chosen. If she is wrong, another clue should be given.

NOW TRY THIS

1. Look at the photos and sort them into matching pairs. For example, you may decide to match people by their features or gender.
2. Stick the photos onto your paper. Join the pairs with a line. Over the top of the line say why you have put the two photos in pairs.

PHOTO SPOT

THINKING SKILL: reasoning, enquiry
SUBJECT LINK: geography
LEARNING LINK: auditory
ORGANISATION: small groups
RESOURCES: photographs taken at various spots around the school grounds, either the same set for each group or 30 different photos – some can be of the same object but taken from a different place; an adult to supervise the group activity outside; a digital camera; paper, pencils and glue

WHAT TO DO

● In your small groups or with a partner, look at the photos and, one at a time, identify what these are and where they can be found in the school grounds.
● Give each of your photos a number so that you know which one you will try to find first, which one second, and so on.

NOW TRY THIS

1. Go outside in your group and find the object in your first photo.
2. When you have found it, look carefully and see if you can work out the exact spot or angle from which the photo was taken.
3. How do you know whether you are right? What clues are you using?
4. Do the same for the other photos.
5. If you can, take another photo of one of your objects to match against the original on return to the classroom.
6. Stick your photos to a large sheet of paper and label with the direction and spot you think the picture was taken from.

ROLE-PLAY RESOURCES

THINKING SKILL: creative thinking, enquiry
SUBJECT LINK: English (speaking and listening), design and technology
LEARNING LINK: auditory
ORGANISATION: group activity
RESOURCES: large sheets of paper; pencils; pictures of seaside environments (the Katie Morag stories are a good source as you may decide to use these as a context)

WHAT TO DO

● Decide, as a group, which place to develop into a seaside role-play area.
● Draw a design for your role-play area. Include the resources you will need and where to put them. Make the area fit the space you have available.
● Label your design so that the resources you need are identified.

NOW TRY THIS

1. Choose a character you might find at the seaside. Talk about what they might wear. Would they have any tools or other resources to show who they are and what they are doing?
2. List the clothes and resources needed for dressing up as that person.

GUESS WHO?

THINKING SKILL: enquiry
SUBJECT LINK: science, English (speaking and listening)
LEARNING LINK: auditory
ORGANISATION: groups
RESOURCES: photographs of everyone in the room displayed on a board

WHAT TO DO

● Look at the photos of your classmates.
● Talk to a friend about the different features some of your classmates have, such as the colour of their hair and eyes.
● Now think about the hair – what style it is, how long it is and who has a ribbon, slide or some other decoration.
● Does anyone wear glasses?
● How many boys/girls are there?

NOW TRY THIS

1. Describe one of the children in the class for your friend to try to guess who it is.

2. Swap over and try to guess who your friend is describing.
3. Agree together what was the most useful piece of information for working out who the person was.
4. What was the least useful piece of information?

> **ANSWERS**
> Good questions are those with only two criteria (for example, boy or girl). This question will mean you know that it isn't almost half of the group. Questions about hair and eye colour will mean eliminating a third or quarter of children, depending on the class. Questions about a particular item such as hair slides or glasses will only be useful if the answer is 'Yes' (fewer children will have these).

GUESS WHO AGAIN?

THINKING SKILL: enquiry, evaluation
SUBJECT LINK: science, English (speaking and listening)
LEARNING LINK: auditory
ORGANISATION: groups
RESOURCES: photographs of everyone in the room, displayed on a board

WHAT TO DO

● Ask one of your group to describe another child in the class from their photograph.
● From their description, think of the questions you could ask to try to guess who they are thinking of. The questions should only invite a 'Yes' or 'No' answer.
● For example, you could ask whether the person is a boy. From the answer, you will be able to eliminate all the boys or all the girls.
● Next you could ask whether the person has blond hair. This will help you eliminate all the children who do or do not have blond hair.
● Which questions will help you to eliminate the most photos? Why?

NOW TRY THIS

1. One of your group thinks of a person. Ask 'Yes' and 'No' questions until you have enough information to guess who that person is thinking of.
2. A wrong guess costs three questions.
3. Try to guess the person in less than ten, and then five, questions.

GUESS THE SOUND

THINKING SKILL: information processing, creative thinking
SUBJECT LINK: music
LEARNING LINK: visual
ORGANISATION: small groups
RESOURCES: a picture containing objects that make sounds such as transport, animals, people, machinery and weather conditions; percussion instruments; pictures from familiar stories, including the Katie Morag stories (for display only)

WHAT TO DO

● Talk about the picture. Name some of the things that make sounds.
● Write down some useful words to describe the sounds.
● Take it in turns to make or describe the sound of one of the objects in the picture for the rest of the group to guess. No actions allowed!
● Keep going until everyone has had two turns.
● Did you find it easier to make or describe the sounds?

NOW TRY THIS

1. Use the musical instruments and objects to make sounds to match objects in the picture. You may not be able to match them exactly, but get as close as you can. Try a soft, loud, scraping, fast, slow, high or low sound.
2. Create a sound picture with the instruments to perform to the class.
3. Listen to other groups' compositions. Make a mental note on how they are the same or different to yours.
4. Talk to your teacher about the musical elements you used to recreate the sounds in the picture.

ANSWERS
Elements include:
1. Texture – the way sounds are combined together.
2. Pitch – the melody or tune and the way it goes up and down.
3. Duration – long and short notes, the pulse and combination of sounds into different beats or rhythms.
4. Dynamics – how loud or quiet it is.
5. Tempo – how fast or slow the music is.
6. Timbre – different types of sound.

SOUND SIGNALS

THINKING SKILL: information processing
SUBJECT LINK: science
ORGANISATION: pairs
RESOURCES: tape of everyday sounds to which the children need to respond (the school bells for lining up, coming into school, evacuating the building, end of lesson, assembly; the start-up sound of the computer; the sound a mobile phone makes when turned on or off and when it receives a text message; the sound a Roamer makes when programmed and when it has finished its manoeuvre); a tape of other sounds familiar from around the school (pedestrian crossing beeps, sirens, burglar alarms, telephone and door bells)

WHAT TO DO

● Listen to the first sound on the tape. Talk about it. What is making it? What is it alerting you to?
● Continue until you have listened to and identified all of the sounds on the tape. Note what each sound is telling you to do.

NOW TRY THIS

Talk about some of the other sounds you hear during school. Make a list of these. Share the list with another pair to create a much bigger list.

RINGTONES

> **THINKING SKILL:** enquiry, evaluation
> **SUBJECT LINK:** science, mathematics
> **LEARNING LINK:** visual
> **ORGANISATION:** pairs, then small groups
> **RESOURCES:** mobile phone ringtones; an adult to play these; paper; pens

WHAT TO DO

● Listen to the first ringtone. Do you like it? How do you make a decision about how much you like it? Is it pleasant to listen to? Is it a favourite tune that reminds you of something? Will you be able to hear it easily so that you can answer the phone quickly? Give the ringtone a mark out of ten.

● Listen to the other ringtones in turn. Give each a mark out of ten, answering the questions above.

● Share your decisions with another pair. Did you have the same favourite?

NOW TRY THIS

1. Put the information onto a chart. Make a graph to show the favourite and least favourite ringtone among your class. Decide which is the best sort of graph. Should you use a computer program?

2. Set up an investigation in science to find out which ringtone can be heard the clearest by most of your class.

POETIC SOUNDS

> **THINKING SKILL:** creative thinking, evaluation
> **SUBJECT LINK:** music, English (speaking and listening)
> **LEARNING LINK:** visual
> **ORGANISATION:** individuals, pairs, then small groups of four
> **RESOURCES:** a poem which conjures up lots of sounds such as 'This is the Key to the Castle' by Dave Caulder from *Twinkle, Twinkle, Chocolate Bar* (Oxford University Press); paper and crayons; musical instruments; a set of poetry books

WHAT TO DO

● Listen to the poem. Draw your own picture of what you can see in your head.

● Share the pictures and talk about the things you can see in each picture in turn. Then talk about the sounds you might hear if you were transported into the pictures.

● Label your pictures with the objects and instruments you could use to recreate the sounds.

NOW TRY THIS

1. Find the objects and instruments you need and turn one of your pictures into a sound poem.
2. In small groups, perform each other's poems – one person reading the poem and the others adding the sounds.

SOUND QUESTIONS

> **THINKING SKILL:** enquiry
> **SUBJECT LINK:** music, science, English (speaking and listening)
> **LEARNING LINK:** visual
> **ORGANISATION:** pairs
> **RESOURCES:** two pictures that contain objects that make different sounds, such as transport, animals, people, machinery and weather conditions

WHAT TO DO

● Talk about the picture. Find as many objects as you can that make a sound.

● Choose one of the objects you have found. Agree the type of sound it would make – for example, loud, soft, fast, high, low, slow.

● List all the words you can think of to describe the object's sound.

● Use these words to think up questions that require a 'Yes' or 'No' answer to try to guess another object from its sound. For example, does the object make a loud sound? Does it make a high, low, fast, quiet, loud, slow, scraping or smooth sound?

● Now play this game:
  1. Ask your friend to think of another object in the picture that makes a sound, keeping it a secret.
  2. Ask your friend a question about the sound. Remember he/she is only allowed to answer 'Yes' or 'No'.
  3. Keep asking the questions until you guess the object.
  4. Swap over roles.

NOW TRY THIS

1. Team up with another pair of children.
2. Select a different picture and use it to play the game as a small group.

MATCHING SOUNDS

THINKING SKILL: information processing, evaluation
SUBJECT LINK: science.
LEARNING LINK: visual, kinaesthetic
ORGANISATION: small groups
RESOURCES: disposable drinking cups; paper and/or fabric cut into squares large enough to cover the top of the cups; elastic bands; dried pulses; paper clips; counters; sand; rice

WHAT TO DO

● Each person in your group should put different objects into drinking cups. Cover the top of each cup with a piece of thin paper or fabric, secured with an elastic band.
● In turn, shake the pots and talk about the sounds produced.
● What made the different sounds? Was it the size, shape, texture, colour or material of the objects inside the pots?
● Did the fuller or emptier pots make the better sound? Why?
● Refill the pots but adjust the amount you put in according to your evaluation.
● Listen to the pots again.

NOW TRY THIS

1. Swap your pot with another child in your group.
2. All of the group should now use the same number and type of objects to make a pot that makes exactly the same sound when it is shaken.
3. Is it easier or harder to do when the things in the pot are the same materials or different?
4. Test out the pots (one pair at a time) and agree when they make matching sounds.
5. Join up with another group. Mix up the pots and play the following game.
6. Take it in turns to shake one pot, replacing it in its place; choose another pot to shake. If it matches then you have won both pots. If it doesn't, return it to the same place for another friend to have a go. The person with the most matching pots is the winner.

TWENTY QUESTIONS

THINKING SKILL: enquiry
SUBJECT LINK: English (speaking and listening)
LEARNING LINK: visual
ORGANISATION: groups of three
RESOURCES: paper and pencils

WHAT TO DO

● Look around the room and choose an object to talk about. Discuss the object, using words to describe its colour, shape, position, texture and what it is used for.
● Identify a few questions that require a 'Yes' or 'No' answer.
● Play a game where the aim is to guess the name of an object chosen by a member of the group using up to 20 questions.
● Give each member of the group a job:
  1. to choose an object;
  2. to ask questions that require a 'Yes' or 'No' answer;
  3. to keep count of the questions.
● The person asking questions can ask up to 20 questions to try to work out the object their friend is thinking about. They are not allowed to guess until they are sure. A wrong guess costs ten questions.
● Swap over roles until you have all had one go at thinking of an object, asking questions and keeping count.
● What was the least number of questions used before someone guessed the answer?
● Why was this?

NOW TRY THIS

1. Use the lowest number of questions asked as a new target for the game. Keep reducing the target until you reach ten questions.
2. What are the most effective questions?

> **ANSWER**
> Encourage the children to start with questions that eliminate half of the items. For example: *Is the object larger than a table?* Also encourage them to ask questions of colour that use their knowledge of colour mixing, for example: *Can its colour be made from two other colours?*

SHARING MUSIC

THINKING SKILL: evaluation
SUBJECT LINK: music, ICT
LEARNING LINK: kinaesthetic
ORGANISATION: whole class
RESOURCES: ask children to bring in a favourite extract of music; tape recorder and/or CD player

WHAT TO DO
- Play one of the pieces.
- Ask the child who chose it to tell the rest of the class why they have chosen this piece.
- How does it make them feel? Does it make them want to dance, go to sleep, sit quietly? Does it make them think of a favourite pastime? Does it make them remember a holiday, a friend, relative or pet?

NOW TRY THIS
1. Listen to someone else's favourite piece of music. Does it conjure up similar feelings and memories to the first piece?
2. How are they the same? Why?
3. List all the things they had in common on one side of a piece of paper and all the different things on the other side.

MAP YOUR LISTENING

THINKING SKILL: reasoning
SUBJECT LINK: music
LEARNING LINK: visual
ORGANISATION: pairs or small groups
RESOURCES: large sheets of paper; pens; recording of *Happy Farmer* by Schumann

WHAT TO DO
- Listen to the piece of music. Write words on the paper to show how it makes you feel, the type of sounds you hear and any instruments you recognise.
- Talk about these with a friend.
- Link any feelings you felt to the sounds that provoked these. Write the reason over the line you have drawn. Link the sound to the instrument that made it and to the feeling and say why you have linked them. Do this for as many sounds, feelings and instruments that you can.
- Share your listening map with another pair.
- Make up a title for the music.

NOW TRY THIS
Repeat the activity with another piece of music.

GIVE IT A TITLE

THINKING SKILL: creative thinking
SUBJECT LINK: music
LEARNING LINK: visual
ORGANISATION: pairs or small groups
RESOURCES: several pieces of music that conjure up a picture, for example, recordings of Tchaikovsky's *Nutcracker Suite*, Mussorgsky's *Pictures from an Exhibition* or Saint Saens' *Carnival of the Animals* or Rimsky-Korsakov's *Flight of the Bumblebee*; paper; pencils

WHAT TO DO
- Listen to the first piece of music.
- Talk together about what you can hear.
- Does the music make a picture in your head?
- Write down a title that you think best describes the music. Write this down as number one on your list.
- Repeat this activity for four more pieces of music. You should end up with five titles on your list.

NOW TRY THIS
1. Ask the children to choose a title and share it with the class. Challenge them to say which piece of music the title is for.
2. Look at the actual titles for each of the pieces of music.
3. How close were their titles?

A NICE ALTERNATIVE

THINKING SKILL: evaluation
SUBJECT LINK: English (literacy)
ORGANISATION: whole class
RESOURCES: a thesaurus; a large sheet of paper and pens; a short description containing only the word 'nice' to describe things

WHAT TO DO

● Read the short extract to the children. Ask them if they noticed whether a word was used too often.
● Find the word 'nice' in the dictionary. Read out its definition.
● Ask the children to think of other words that could be used instead of 'nice'. For example, a nice person could also be a friendly person.
● Write down all the words that the children can think of. You may wish to include the context or subject in brackets; for example, friendly (person).
● Introduce a thesaurus to find other words for 'nice'.

NOW TRY THIS

1. Read the extract again, but this time substitute each 'nice' with an alternative word from the list.
2. Ask the children which version they preferred. Give both versions a mark out of ten.
3. Ask them to write their own short extracts that use the idea of someone or something being nice (but not using the word 'nice').

SOUND SNAP

THINKING SKILL: information processing
SUBJECT LINK: music, science
LEARNING LINK: visual
ORGANISATION: small groups or whole class
RESOURCES: two identical sets of musical instruments and objects that make a sound; two identical drums and a range of different types of beaters – soft-headed, wire, plastic, rubber, wood and metal

WHAT TO DO

● Look at the instruments and objects.
● Choose one of the instruments and make a sound. How did you make the sound? Can you produce a different sound on the same instrument by playing it a different way?
● Invite another person to use the identical instrument and to reproduce the sound exactly.
● Was the sound produced the same type, loudness, speed and pitch?
● Divide your group into two. Sit the two groups back-to-back in a line with the instruments and objects in front of them.
● Take it in turns for one person in the first group to make a sound for the person sitting back-to-back with them in the second group to reproduce exactly. The group copying can talk about the sound and instrument or object used, although only one person should play the sound. Continue until everyone has had a go.

ALPHABET MAGIC

THINKING SKILL: information processing, enquiry
SUBJECT LINK: English (literacy)
LEARNING LINK: visual
ORGANISATION: pairs and then small groups
RESOURCES: reference books, dictionaries, atlases and maps; paper and pens; alphabet frieze

WHAT TO DO

● Choose a letter from the alphabet and answer these questions:
  1. Does it come near the start, middle or end of the alphabet?
  2. Which letter comes before and after it?
  3. Does the letter appear in your names?
  4. Does the letter appear in the school name?
  5. Think of ten more things you can say about the letter.
● Do the same thing with three more letters.

NOW TRY THIS

1. For each of the letters you have chosen, think of the name of a flower, animal, fruit, vegetable, insect and bird, starting with these letters.
2. Try to find the name of a country, river, town or city that starts with this letter. Use maps and reference books.
3. Which letter did you find easiest/hardest?

FIND THE LETTER

THINKING SKILL: information processing
SUBJECT LINK: English (literacy)
LEARNING LINK: visual
ORGANISATION: pairs
RESOURCES: dictionaries that have an alphabet on each page with the letter that starts the words on the page highlighted

WHAT TO DO

● Look at a dictionary, and talk with a partner about the way the words are organised.
● Which letter comes first in the book?
● Which comes last?
● Is there an alphabet at the top, bottom or somewhere else on each page?
● Which letter is highlighted?
● What does this help you do?
● Read the alphabet together out loud. Listen to the sound of each letter. Try to remember the order of all the letters.

NOW TRY THIS

1. Try to open the dictionary at the word 'magic'. Say the letter that begins the word out loud. Does this word start with a letter at the beginning, end or middle of the alphabet? Where will you open the dictionary?
2. Do this again for the words 'seaside', 'ant', 'violin' and 'grapes'.

FOLLOW THE LINES

THINKING SKILL: information processing
SUBJECT LINK: mathematics, English (handwriting)
LEARNING LINK: kinaesthetic
ORGANISATION: individuals
RESOURCES: sheets of A4 or A3 paper with a large pound sign drawn on for each child; crayons or felt-tipped pens; *Skaters' Waltz* by Tchaikovsky

WHAT TO DO

● Listen to the music once, looking at the shape of the pound sign at the same time. Count the four beats to the tune. Think how the drawing of the sign can fit into the music.
● Trace over the sign with your finger in time to the music. This will help you find a flow to your movements. Draw over the top to the first beat, down to the second, loop and across to the third and add the two horizontal lines to the fourth.

● Choose a coloured crayon and draw over the sign in time to the music.
● Choose a different colour and repeat tracing over the sign until you have produced a rainbow-coloured pound sign.

NOW TRY THIS

Choose a different sign, letter or number that you need to learn the formation for and repeat the activity. The letters **a**, **d**, **g**, **q** and the number **9** are good because the formation fits the music.

HAND JIVE

THINKING SKILL: creative thinking
SUBJECT LINK: music
LEARNING LINK: kinaesthetic
ORGANISATION: whole class or groups
RESOURCES: a piece of eight- or 16-beat music (1950s and 1960s music (vet the words first) or country dance music)

WHAT TO DO

● Listen to the piece of music. Clap the beat.
● Count how many beats there are before the music repeats itself.
● Listen to the music again. Add some different actions such as tapping your knees, clicking your fingers, tapping the top of one clenched hand with the other (and vice versa) and touching each elbow with the opposite hand.
● Include combinations – for example, two claps, two slaps on the knees, right hand over left twice, left hand over right twice, and so on. Then increase the repeats to four.

NOW TRY THIS

1. Work with a group to create a sequence of actions to fit the music. Do two of each action until the music repeats its beat. Repeat the actions.
2. Perform your hand jive to the rest of the class.

WHAT'S THE MATTER?

THINKING SKILL: enquiry, evaluation, creative thinking
SUBJECT LINK: PSHE
LEARNING LINK: visual
ORGANISATION: small groups
RESOURCES: pictures from, or a copy of, the story of Jack and the Beanstalk

WHAT TO DO

- Listen to the story. Look at the pictures.
- Think about these questions:
  1. *Should Jack have climbed the beanstalk?*
  2. *Should he have stolen?*
  3. *Should the giant have behaved as he did?*
  4. *What sort of character does the giant's wife have?*
  5. *What is Jack's mother like?*
  6. *Who is the naughtiest person in the story? Why?*
  7. *Who is the nicest? Why?*

NOW TRY THIS

1. Put together a short play to persuade Jack not to steal and the giant to be nice to Jack.
2. Act this out for the class. What do they think of your play?

WHAT'S THE NUMBER?

THINKING SKILL: enquiry, reasoning
SUBJECT LINK: mathematics
LEARNING LINK: visual (if 100-squares are used)
ORGANISATION: pairs or small groups
RESOURCES: paper and pencils; 100-squares (optional)

WHAT TO DO

- Think of a number between 1 and 49. Write this on your piece of paper. Write down all the things you know about this number. For example, is it odd or even? Is it larger or smaller than 25, 10, 20? Is it a multiple of 3, 5, 10?
- List the questions requiring a 'Yes' or 'No' answer you would ask to guess this number.

- Number the questions in the order that you would ask them.
- Try to play the following game without using a 100-square (but use one if it helps).
- One of you thinks of a number between 1 and 49. The other one asks the questions in the order you have decided.
- Did you guess the number?
- How many questions did you need to ask?

NOW TRY THIS

1. Play the game again and see if you can guess the number using just five questions.
2. Re-organise the order of the questions if necessary.
3. Try to guess a number between 1 and 99 in fewer than ten questions.

ANSWERS
Good questions to ask:
1. Is it an odd number? (because it reduces the numbers it can be by half)
2. Does it come before 40 and after 20? (because it narrows down by half again the rest of the search)
3. (Depending on the answer to question 2) – Does it come before 15 or 35 and after 5 or 25?
4. Does it end in the digit 6 (or 5 if the answer to the first question is 'Yes')?
5. Is it a multiple of 5 (or 3, 4 or 6)?

KERRY'S GAME

THINKING SKILL: information processing
SUBJECT LINK: science
LEARNING LINK: visual
ORGANISATION: small groups
RESOURCES: a tray for each group containing ten different objects from around the classroom, some of which have the same properties, uses, colour, shape and material; a timer to set one, two and five minutes

WHAT TO DO

- Look at the objects. Talk to a friend about what you can see. After five minutes you will be asked to remember all of the objects.
- Talk about which objects have something in common, such as the same colour, shape, use or material.

● Can you pair up the objects so that if you remember one you automatically remember the other?

● After five minutes, cover the tray with a cloth. You now have one minute to name out loud all of the objects. How many did you remember?

NOW TRY THIS

1. Move to another group and look at the objects on the tray. You have two minutes to quickly identify the things that are the same about this set of objects.

2. Cover the tray and see how many objects you can remember in one minute.

LEARN A NEW SONG

THINKING SKILL: information processing
SUBJECT LINK: music
LEARNING LINK: visual
ORGANISATION: whole class
RESOURCES: a tape of a short song that includes an easily recollected chorus (have a separate recording of the chorus or note where this is on the tape so that you can find it quickly. If you have the skills, lead the echo singing. If not, ask a colleague to record the first verse so that the first line is sung through twice without stopping, then the second line and so on to the end of the verse. You can turn on the tape and let the children follow it without stopping); typewritten words on an OHP or whiteboard screen

WHAT TO DO

● Listen to the song and talk about the things you remember. Share these with the class.

● Can you remember any of the chorus?

● Listen to the song again and this time listen out for the parts you remember and try to note new things. Join in with as much of the chorus as you can.

● Listen to the chorus on its own and then join in when it is played again.

● Learn the first verse by echo singing. You

may need to do this twice. Listen to the whole song again and join in with the first verse and the chorus until everyone knows it.

NOW TRY THIS

1. Look at the words of the second verse.

2. The class will be split into two groups. The first group will sing the first line of the second verse for the second group to copy.

3. Repeat this for the second line, then the third, until you have echo sung the whole of the verse.

4. Sing the chorus together.

5. Repeat, but swap over so that the first group sings the echo part.

6. Sing as much of the song as you can along with the tape.

RHYMING RHYTHMS

THINKING SKILL: information processing
SUBJECT LINK: music
LEARNING LINK: kinaesthetic
ORGANISATION: groups or whole class
RESOURCES: none

WHAT TO DO

● Think about the nursery rhymes and other rhymes that you know.

● Sing some of these through as a class.

● Your teacher will choose one rhyme with a distinctive rhythm such as 'Jack and Jill'.

● Sing this again, clapping the rhythm as you sing.

● Repeat the rhyme but only clap the rhythm. Sing the words in your head.

● Choose another rhyme and clap the rhythm to it, singing the words in your head.

NOW TRY THIS

1. Take it in turns to clap the rhythm of a familiar rhyme or song that you all know. Sing the words in your head to help you.

2. The rest of the group will try to guess which rhyme or song is being clapped.

FEELINGS

THINKING SKILL: reasoning

SUBJECT LINK: science, English (speaking and listening)

LEARNING LINK: kinaesthetic

ORGANISATION: whole-class introduction, then groups of six

RESOURCES: enough boxes or bags for each group to have one (each box or bag should hold one object that has a distinctive texture, use or shape such as an orange, a large piece of cotton wool, an ice cube wrapped in bubble wrap, a large metal spoon, sandpaper, a cabasa, a toothbrush)

WHAT TO DO

● Ask one child to feel the object in the box or bag.

● Ask them to describe the object without saying what it is, thinking about the object's size, shape, use and texture. When they have finished, the rest of the class try to guess what the object is.

NOW TRY THIS

1. Each group will have a bag or box containing an object.

2. Choose someone to describe what is in the bag or box by feeling it.

3. When they have finished their description, say what you think is in the box or bag.

4. Were you right?

5. How did the description help you? Which bit of information was the most useful?

6. Swap your box or bag with another group.

TOWERS

THINKING SKILL: enquiry, reasoning

SUBJECT LINK: English (speaking and listening)

LEARNING LINK: kinaesthetic

ORGANISATION: pairs

RESOURCES: multi-link cubes that will join in more than one place; a screen (a large book will do)

WHAT TO DO

● Put the screen or large book between you and your partner so that you cannot see what the other one is doing. Take enough of the same coloured cubes to make two towers ten cubes high.

● One of you now picks up a cube, telling your partner what colour it is. Your partner should now pick up a cube of the same colour.

● Pick up another cube, telling your partner the colour and how you are fixing it to the first cube to start your tower.

● Repeat this until you have both made a ten-cube tower.

● Remove the screen and see if the towers are identical.

● Repeat with the first person building the tower and the second person copying.

NOW TRY THIS

1. Make a different model with your cubes. Don't tell your partner what the model will be, although as you fix each cube describe precisely where you are fixing it. Add a few more cubes on top, below and to the side, describing what you do.

2. After fixing six cubes, remove the screen and see if your friend's model is the same.

> **ANSWERS**
> Encourage the children to use precise positional language – for example, on top, to the right or left side, fixed to the right or left side of the second cube from the bottom.

HEARING INFERENCE

THINKING SKILL: reasoning

SUBJECT LINK: English (literacy)

LEARNING LINK: visual

ORGANISATION: whole class or groups

RESOURCES: a copy of *A Wolf at the Door* by Nick Ward (Scholastic) or an alternative book; paper, pencils and crayons

WHAT TO DO

● Start to read the story to the children, adding the sound effects when you get to the first knock at the door.

● Read the reply in character to give the children a clue as to who may be at the door.

● Ask the children at this point to guess who it is. Read on to find out if they are correct.

● Continue to read, and identify the inference in the descriptions which helps to guess the next characters to appear – the Three Little Pigs and Little Bo Peep.

● Show the children the pictures from the next part of the story to help them infer that Red Riding Hood, Cinderella and Goldilocks come to the door next.

NOW TRY THIS

1. Read the description of the wolf. Give the children ten minutes to draw what they think he looks like.

2. Share a few pictures before showing them the illustrator's imaginary picture.

3. Read the end of the story showing them which wolf is at the door. Talk about whether the characters had been imagining things. Read the final sentence. What do the children think now?

MUSICAL FEELINGS

THINKING SKILL: evaluation
SUBJECT LINK: PSHE, citizenship
LEARNING LINK: visual
ORGANISATION: small groups or pairs
RESOURCES: a large sheet of paper for each group; felt-tipped pens; a CD player; two very different extracts of music, one quiet and gentle such as Pachebel's *Canon in D Major* and the other lively and discordant such as Rimsky-Korsakov's *Flight of the Bumblebee*.

WHAT TO DO

● Listen to the first piece of music quietly by yourself for two minutes.

● Close your eyes. Conjure up a picture in your mind from the music.

● Talk with a partner about how the music makes you feel.

● Does it make you feel calm, happy, sad and so on?

● Share the picture that you saw in your mind.

NOW TRY THIS

1. Listen to the second piece of music for two minutes, thinking about how this makes you feel and the picture it creates in your head.

2. When your group is ready, write words, draw patterns and pictures of how the music makes you feel.

3. Talk as a class about what the composer

has done to create such emotions and pictures. Think about how the instruments are put together to create the atmosphere, how the volume, speed, rhythms and tempo are changed.

4. Now listen to the first piece of music again.

5. Turn your paper over and write, draw patterns and pictures of how it makes you feel.

6. Talk to your friends about how the composer has used the tune, tempo, number and way the instruments are played to create atmosphere.

GLOSSARY SHAPES

THINKING SKILL: information processing
SUBJECT LINK: mathematics
LEARNING LINK: visual, kinaesthetic
ORGANISATION: pairs
RESOURCES: paper and pencils; descriptions of shapes; 3-D shapes

WHAT TO DO

● Your teacher will describe a shape – for example, it has four sides, all the sides are the same length, it has four right angles.

● Listen carefully and draw the shape you think is being described.

● Your teacher will repeat the description. Listen to check whether you have drawn precisely what is being described.

● Work in pairs to each describe and draw a shape you like. Make sure you describe the shape well enough for your partner to draw.

● Label the shape's properties:

1. Describe the length of its sides and their position to each other.

2. Describe the size of its angles and their position to each other.

3. Write down the description.

● Read your descriptions to another pair. Ask them to draw the shape.

● Does the shape they have drawn match yours? Swap over. Listen to the other pair's descriptions and draw the shape.

NOW TRY THIS

1. Think of descriptions for a range of 3-D shapes.

2. Challenge your partner to find, for example, the shape that has one square face and four triangular faces.

LISTEN AND DRAW

THINKING SKILL: information processing
SUBJECT LINK: science, art and design
LEARNING LINK: visual, kinaesthetic
ORGANISATION: small groups, then pairs
RESOURCES: a collection of leaves with a distinctive shape, size, texture or number of leaflets, such as sycamore, holly, ash, horse chestnut and oak; unusual leaves from flowers; sorting rings; paper or card for labels; pens, paper, pencils

WHAT TO DO

● Look at the leaves and talk about all the properties you can see and feel – for example, the colour, shape, number of leaflets, size and texture.
● Next identify the features such as stem or stalk, veins, edges, top and underside.
● Sort the leaves into sets. Label each set.

NOW TRY THIS

1. With a friend, choose a leaf. Talk about it together until you are clear about its shape, size, features and texture.
2. Hide the leaf somewhere so that you cannot see it.
3. Both of you try to draw the leaf exactly as you remember it.
4. Compare your drawings with each other's and then with the actual leaf.
5. How close were you? Did talking about its properties help?
6. Talk about the colours in the leaf. Colour your drawing as close to its actual colours as you can.

LISTEN AND MATCH

THINKING SKILL: reasoning
SUBJECT LINK: science
LEARNING LINK: visual
ORGANISATION: small groups
RESOURCES: an identical set of photographs of natural objects for each group; a large sheet of paper; pens

WHAT TO DO

● Spread out the photos on the table.
● Each group member should choose a photograph by looking, not by touching. Keep the one you have chosen a secret.
● Take it in turns to give a clue as to what is in the photograph without saying its name.

● The child sitting to your right should say which photograph he thinks is being described. If right, he should then give a clue to the photograph he has chosen. If wrong, another clue should be given.

NOW TRY THIS

1. Look at the photographs and sort them into matching pairs. For example, by the objects' colour, shape, texture, where they are found, and so on.
2. Stick the photographs onto your sheet of paper and join the pairs with a line. Over the top of the line, write the reason you have matched them.

LISTEN AND MAP

THINKING SKILL: reasoning
SUBJECT LINK: science, English (literacy)
LEARNING LINK: visual
ORGANISATION: small groups
RESOURCES: large sheets of paper; pencils; a variety of objects such as a plant (with or without flowers), shell, wooden branch, stone or rock, and a clear glass object

WHAT TO DO

● Look at the object in the centre of your table.
● Talk about it with your group, and say as many words as you can to describe that object. Think about how to spell the words as you say them.
● Place the object in the centre of the large sheet of paper and, as a group, write down all the words you found to describe the object.
● Draw lines from each word to the object. How many have you found?

NOW TRY THIS

Use a line and join words with others that will link in some way. For example, match a colour with its feature, or a shape with its position. Take turns in linking words, and explain why you are linking them as you draw the line.

MY HOBBY

THINKING SKILL: enquiry
SUBJECT LINK: English (speaking and listening)
LEARNING LINK: visual
ORGANISATION: whole-class presentation or circle time
RESOURCES: will vary depending on presentations

WHAT TO DO

● Think of something you really like to do.
● Think about the things you use, the things you do and the people you meet.
● Put together a one-minute presentation of your favourite pastime using photographs, medals you may have won, toys you play with or a video you have made.

NOW TRY THIS

1. Present your hobby or pastime to the rest of the class. Take no more than a minute for this.
2. Include a question-and-answer session.

WHO IS RIGHT?

THINKING SKILL: enquiry
SUBJECT LINK: history
LEARNING LINK: visual
ORGANISATION: small groups
RESOURCES: a set of household objects used in Victorian times that are not used today and don't look like today's objects (for example, a button hook, butter churn, bed warmer); photocopies from reference books which explain what each object was used for (or explanations written by the teacher)

WHAT TO DO

● Talk about your object.
● Decide together what it could have been used for.
● Use the ideas to write a short description of what you think the object was used for.

● Now read what it was really used for. Were you right? Use the information to write down another (correct) description.

NOW TRY THIS

Each group should present their two descriptions to the rest of the class. The class should choose which one is correct.

LEARN FROM A SONG

THINKING SKILL: information processing
SUBJECT LINK: music
LEARNING LINK: visual
ORGANISATION: whole class
RESOURCES: labels with days of the week and months of the year

WHAT TO DO

● Learn the song 'Ten Little Indians':

> *One little, two little, three little Indians*
> *Four little, five little, six little Indians*
> *Seven little, eight little, nine little Indians*
> *Ten little Indian boys.*

● Sing it through twice until you are familiar with the tune.

NOW TRY THIS

1. Change the words so that you are singing the days of the week:

> *There's Sunday, and Monday, and Tuesday, and Wednesday,*
> *Then Thursday, then Friday, the last day is Saturday;*
> *One, two, three, four, five, six and seven days,*
> *Seven days are in a week.*

2. Choose children to stand up with labels of the days of the week in the right order as the song is sung.

DRAW WHAT YOU HEAR

THINKING SKILL: information processing
SUBJECT LINK: English (speaking and listening)
LEARNING LINK: visual
ORGANISATION: whole class with children working individually
RESOURCES: a copy of *A Wolf at the Door* by Nick Ward (Scholastic) or another picture book familiar to the children that has a picture easy enough for them to draw

WHAT TO DO

● Your teacher will read the opening of the story.
● He or she will read the first sentence and describe what he/she can see in the picture.
● Draw what you hear. Make sure you think about the position and colour of the objects.
● Think from what you have heard what may be seen through the window.

NOW TRY THIS

1. With a friend, find a favourite story starter you think would be good for the class to draw what they hear.
2. Talk about how you would describe the picture so that they could draw an accurate match for it.
3. With another pair, take it in turns to describe and draw a story starter.

NICE SOUNDS OR NOT

THINKING SKILL: information processing, reasoning, enquiry, evaluation
SUBJECT LINK: geography
LEARNING LINK: visual
ORGANISATION: small groups
RESOURCES: a collection of nice sounds and not so nice sounds collected from the local area such as traffic noises, birds singing, babies crying, water gurgling, people shouting, people singing; a map of the local area; paper; pencils

WHAT TO DO

● On your own, listen quietly to all of the sounds on the tape. Identify as many as you can.

● Listen to the sounds again. Talk to a friend. Agree which sounds are nice and which are not so nice. Give reasons.

NOW TRY THIS

1. Join together with two other pairs. Sort the sounds into two columns: one nice and the other not so nice.
2. Use drawings, pictures from magazines or words to make a note of other sounds.
3. Which is the nicest sound and which is the least nice sound? Give reasons.
4. Talk about what you could do to make the least nice sound more pleasant.

WHERE WOULD YOU HEAR THIS?

THINKING SKILL: information processing, reasoning, enquiry, evaluation
SUBJECT LINK: geography
LEARNING LINK: visual
ORGANISATION: pairs
RESOURCES: a collection of sounds from the local area such as traffic sounds, pedestrian crossings, factory noise, children in a playground, swings squeaking, balls bouncing, and church bells or mosque call to prayer; a map of the local area; pencils

WHAT TO DO

● Look at the map of the local area. Agree the sounds you might be able to hear if you walked around.
● Share your ideas with the rest of your group to see if they can guess where your sounds are.

NOW TRY THIS

1. Listen to the first sound on the tape.
2. Look at the map of the local area. Where may this sound have been recorded?
3. Write the number 1 in this place.
4. Listen to the second sound. Where may this sound have been recorded? Write number 2 on the map. Continue with all the sounds.

LIFE CYCLES

THINKING SKILL: information processing
SUBJECT LINK: science
LEARNING LINK: visual
ORGANISATION: whole class
RESOURCES: a copy of 'I Went to the Cabbages' by Tom Stanier and Liz Bennett from *Tinderbox* (A&C Black); paper; crayons

WHAT TO DO

- Learn the song about the life cycle of the butterfly.
- Draw what you are singing in a circle to show the cycle of life.

NOW TRY THIS

1. Change the words to explain the life cycle of a frog.
2. Here is one example:

> *I went to the local pond one day*
> *What do you think I saw?*
> *Eggs just like jelly, shaped like a welly*
> *(clustered like a jelly, just like seen on telly)*
> *What could it all be for?*
> *Tadpoles' heads like a nail (or whale!), no legs just a tail*
> *Tadpoles now have back legs, eating other frogs' eggs*
> *Frogs jumping here and frogs jumping there.*

SOUND DOMINOES

THINKING SKILL: information processing
SUBJECT LINK: science
LEARNING LINK: kinaesthetic
ORGANISATION: small groups
RESOURCES: several objects that make a sound by tapping, blowing or shaking such as empty crisp packets, a saucepan when struck, wooden objects, bells, whistles, paper being shaken, rustled or torn, clocks ticking; a table top; blank labels; pens

WHAT TO DO

- Listen to the range of sounds made by the different objects. Write words on the labels to describe the sounds such as quiet, tinkling, loud, harsh, and clangy.

NOW TRY THIS

1. Choose an object and decide which sound it makes.

2. Find another object that makes a matching sound. It doesn't have to be exact, just make the same kind of sound – for example, 'tinkly'.
3. Put the second object a short distance from the first. Link the two with a label describing the type of sound both objects make.
4. Continue until you have made a circle.
5. If you get stuck, make lines across the circle like spokes of a wheel.

WIND CHIMES

THINKING SKILL: reasoning
SUBJECT LINK: science
LEARNING LINK: kinaesthetic, visual
ORGANISATION: groups
RESOURCES: wind chimes made from a range of materials including metal, wood, plastic and glass; large sheets of paper; pencils

WHAT TO DO

- Listen to the sound made by each of the wind chimes in turn. Tell a partner which chime sound you like best.
- Listen to the metal chimes. List all the words that describe the sound they make.
- Do the same for the wooden, glass and plastic chimes.

NOW TRY THIS

1. Look at the words for each of the chimes. Highlight the ones that appear in all of the lists.
2. Now find those that appear in three and two lists.
3. Decide which chimes make the clearest sounds and which make the dullest sounds. Which materials are these? Put your chimes in order from the clearest to the dullest. Compare your decisions with another group.
4. Look at some of the tuned percussion instruments in your collection. From what materials are these made? Why are no instruments made from glass? Why are no tuned percussion instruments made from plastic?

GETTING LOST

THINKING SKILL: evaluation
SUBJECT LINK: religious education, English (speaking and listening)
ORGANISATION: whole class
RESOURCES: a copy of the story of Jesus at the Temple found in a children's Bible (Luke 2: 22–52)

WHAT TO DO

● Read the extract from a children's Bible or story until you reach the point where Mary and Joseph could not find Jesus when they were ready to go home to Nazareth from Jerusalem.
● Ask the class how they think Mary and Joseph felt. Why do they think they were worried?
● How do they think Mary and Joseph must have felt after three days?
● Finish the story.

NOW TRY THIS

1. Explore with the children the times when they have become lost. What should they do?
2. Ask whether they have ever gone off without telling their parents where they were going. Explore what happened, and why. Talk about the feelings involved at these times both by the parents and the children.
3. Make a list of dos and don'ts for what to do should children become separated from their parents.

HOW OLD?

THINKING SKILL: reasoning
SUBJECT LINK: mathematics, English (speaking and listening)
LEARNING LINK: visual, kinaesthetic
ORGANISATION: individuals or pairs
RESOURCES: a copy of *Katie Morag and the Birthdays* by Mairi Hedderwick (Bodley Head), read before carrying out the activity; a number line; pictures of the characters

WHAT TO DO

● Talk with a friend about how old Katie Morag could be. She keeps her age a secret but she is older than her brother Liam and sister Flora.

● List all the characters in the book that you know. By the side, write down whether they are older or younger than Katie Morag.
● Write the actual ages if you know them. Guess if you do not know.

NOW TRY THIS

1. Write clues to help others in your class work out how old each character is. For example, to work out the age of Katie's brother you could say: *If Katie Morag is 11 and Liam is three years younger, how old is he?* Place the characters on the number line to help you.
2. Take it in turns to read out a clue for the rest of the class to work out the age of one of your characters.

SING IT OUT LOUD

THINKING SKILL: information processing, reasoning
SUBJECT LINK: English (literacy)
LEARNING LINK: visual
ORGANISATION: whole class
RESOURCES: lists of words with onset and rimes the class are currently learning; knowledge of the tune 'Bingo' (you can hear the tune at www.scoutsongs.com/lyrics/bingo.html)

WHAT TO DO

● Remind the children what onset and rime are.
● Say a few cvc (consonant – vowel – consonant) words and ask the children to identify the onset and rime for each.
● Say the word and then the onset and rime. For example, bat – b and at; cat – c and at; that – th and at, and so on.
● Learn the tune to 'Bingo' using the words:
I know a simple spelling game
for learning rime and onset:
bat <clap> b and at;
cat <clap> c and at;
that <clap> th and at
and that's the way we play it.

NOW TRY THIS

1. Divide the class into two groups. Sing the verse together and when you get to the chorus, ask one half to sing the onset and the other half to sing the rime.
2. Use -and, -ing and -ould for the rimes.

WHAT AM I DESCRIBING?

THINKING SKILL: creative thinking, reasoning, evaluation
SUBJECT LINK: English (speaking and listening)
LEARNING LINK: visual
ORGANISATION: pairs
RESOURCES: pieces of paper; pencils

WHAT TO DO

- Choose any object in the environment.
- Describe it to a friend.
- If your friend does not guess the object quickly, give them a clue.
- Talk together about what was the most useful part of the description. For example, was it the colour, size, shape, material or use?
- Let your friend have a turn.

LISTEN AND MAKE

THINKING SKILL: information processing
SUBJECT LINK: design and technology
LEARNING LINK: kinaesthetic
ORGANISATION: individuals
RESOURCES: one sheet of A4 paper and A3 cut in half horizontally for each child; staplers and staples

WHAT TO DO

- Read the following instructions to the children:

   1. Place your piece of paper in front of you with the short side nearest to you.
   2. Fold about two centimetres over from the bottom.
   3. Turn the paper over.
   4. Fold another two centimetres up.
   5. Turn the paper over.
   6. Fold the paper over again.
   7. Continue until you have reached the top.
   8. Staple one end of the folded paper into place.
   9. Open up the paper to make a fan.

NOW TRY THIS

1. Work out how to make a zigzag book.
2. To do this, try folding the paper in the same way as described above, but make the folds wider.

WHERE AM I GOING?

THINKING SKILL: creative thinking, enquiry
SUBJECT LINK: geography
LEARNING LINK: visual
ORGANISATION: groups
RESOURCES: a playmat map with roads and buildings, or a large map of the local area, for each group; a selection of small-world toys (cars and people)

WHAT TO DO

- Identify all the places of interest on your map.
- Choose a starting and finishing place.
- Instruct one member of your group to move one of the cars or people from one place to the other, giving them directions such as *turn left, go straight ahead* and *then turn right after the tree*. As one person gives directions and another follows them, the rest of the group should check whether they think the route is correct. Is there more than one route?
- Take it in turns to choose a route and give directions, to follow the directions and to act as checker.

COUNTING SONGS

THINKING SKILL: information processing
SUBJECT LINK: mathematics
LEARNING LINK: visual, kinaesthetic
ORGANISATION: whole class
RESOURCES: a copy of 'Two in a Boat', a traditional American song from *Count Me In* (A&C Black); a large space

WHAT TO DO

- Learn the song and put rowing actions to the words.
- The first pair should be side by side. The second pair should get in behind, the third behind those and so on.
- After each verse, work out the table fact.

NOW TRY THIS

Change the numbers getting into the boat so that you are counting in fives, threes and fours.

TRIANGLES

THINKING SKILL: creative thinking
SUBJECT LINK: mathematics
LEARNING LINK: visual
ORGANISATION: individuals, pairs
RESOURCES: a large sheet of paper for each pair or individual; a large collection of different triangles including equilateral, isosceles, right-angled and scalene

WHAT TO DO

● Use the triangles to create pictures with new shapes and objects.
● Share the pictures with a partner and take a photograph.

NOW TRY THIS

1. Use two equilateral triangles. How many shapes and objects can you make? Are the sides touching along the whole side, or just part of it? Are only the corners touching?
2. Draw the shapes you have made.
3. Use two isosceles triangles and make a new set of shapes and pictures. Which parts of the triangles are touching?
4. Use two right-angled triangles to make other shapes and pictures. Which parts of the shapes are touching?

POSSIBLE ANSWERS

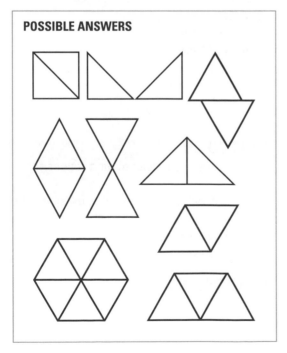

WALKING PENCIL

THINKING SKILL: creative thinking
SUBJECT LINK: English (handwriting), art and design
LEARNING LINK: visual
ORGANISATION: individuals or small groups
RESOURCES: A4 sheets of paper; felt-tipped pens, pencils and wax crayons

WHAT TO DO

● Choose a dark-coloured pencil or pen and take it for a walk around the page, starting at one edge and finishing at another. Go all over the page. It does not matter if you have to cross your path. You want to divide the page into lots of sections.

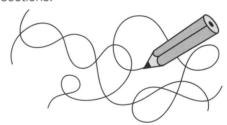

● Choose any colours and fill in each section with a pattern. Do not colour in the whole part, as this will take too long. You could use wavy lines, dots, crosses, straight lines, criss-cross lines, zigzags, or a mixture of all of these.

NOW TRY THIS

Use a ruler to make a straight-line pattern in the same way. Try vertical, horizontal and diagonal lines.

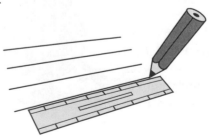

COVER THE PAGE

THINKING SKILL: creative thinking
SUBJECT LINK: mathematics, art
LEARNING LINK: visual
ORGANISATION: individuals
RESOURCES: a poster or wrapping paper that shows tessellating objects such as fish, butterflies or birds; a photocopy of the same poster cut into smaller sections (enough for a few pieces per child); large sheets of paper; scissors; sticky tape; pencils

WHAT TO DO

● Look at the poster. What object has been used to make a tessellating pattern?
● Trace around the outline of the object with your finger.
● Talk to a partner. How were these objects drawn to allow them to fit together?
● Use a square or rectangular shape. On a sheet of paper, make a mark just below the top corner of the shape and just above the bottom corner on the same side.
● Cut a simple shape from this one side, by cutting towards the centre of the shape, starting at one mark and finishing at the other.
● Stick the shape you have cut out to the opposite side with sticky tape to make a new shape.
● Use this new shape to make a small tessellating pattern.
● Did you succeed?

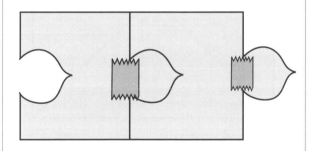

SIDES AND CORNERS

THINKING SKILL: reasoning
SUBJECT LINK: mathematics
LEARNING LINK: visual
ORGANISATION: small groups and pairs
RESOURCES: straws; paper; pencils; an adult to explain how to count corners

WHAT TO DO

● Use three straws and make a shape. How many sides and how many corners are there?
● Use straws to make a square and rectangle. How many straws did you use? How many sides and how many corners does each shape have?
● Use straws to make shapes with five and six sides and corners. How many different shapes have you made? Share your ideas with a partner.
● What do you notice about the number of sides and corners?
● Is there always the same number? Which shapes have a different number of corners to sides? Show an adult.

NOW TRY THIS

1. Work with a partner to make a shape that has more sides than corners.
2. When you think you have done this, make a shape with more corners than sides. Show the shapes to an adult.

> **ANSWER**
> It is not possible to make a shape that has more sides than corners. The children may think there are more sides if the corners they make are inwards rather than outwards from the edge. Explain that a corner is an angle created when two sides meet.

MAKE A MODEL

THINKING SKILL: creative thinking
SUBJECT LINK: design and technology
LEARNING LINK: visual
ORGANISATION: pairs or individuals
RESOURCES: paper and pencils; one tube; one cuboid cardboard box; six circles of card; A4 sheet of card; scissors; PVA glue; sticky tape

WHAT TO DO

● Look at the things in your collection. Design a model that will use all of them.
● Share your idea with a partner. Listen to their idea.
● Choose an idea and make it together, or both of you make your own model.

NOW TRY THIS

1. Think up another set of materials. Challenge a partner to make a different model.
2. Write out the list to use another day.

MAKE A PICTURE

THINKING SKILL: creative thinking
SUBJECT LINK: art and design
LEARNING LINK: visual
ORGANISATION: individuals
RESOURCES: A4 and A3 sheets of paper (one each); print of a Kandinsky painting or a similar piece of art; a range of coloured papers and pens; scissors and glue; crayons and felt-tipped pens

WHAT TO DO

● Look at the Kandinsky painting and name the colours and shapes.
● Try out some of your own ideas on an A4 sheet of paper.
● Experiment with shapes and colours, using crayons and felt-tipped pens.

NOW TRY THIS

1. Cut out some of your shapes from coloured paper.
2. Arrange the shapes on the A3 paper.
3. Stick down your shapes. Add coloured lines with crayon and felt-tipped pens to make a picture like the artist's.
4. Talk about your picture with a partner.

SEEING SHAPES

THINKING SKILL: creative thinking
SUBJECT LINK: art and design
LEARNING LINK: visual
ORGANISATION: individuals and pairs
RESOURCES: print by Miro; black crayons, pens and/or pencils; A3 white paper

WHAT TO DO

● Look at the print by Miro.
● Talk about the shapes he created.
● Take a black crayon, pen or pencil for a wiggly walk, finishing the walk at the same place you started.

● Fill your paper with wiggly line shapes.
● Talk to your partner about the shapes you have each made. Consider what they look like. Do they look like an animal, plant or building?
● Turn your shapes into pictures of animals, plants or other objects.

NOW TRY THIS

1. Use the back of your paper. Draw some wiggly shapes.
2. Swap your paper with a partner and turn their patterns into objects.

TANGRAMS

THINKING SKILL: creative thinking
SUBJECT LINK: mathematics
LEARNING LINK: visual
ORGANISATION: small groups or pairs
RESOURCES: tangram shapes (enough for each pair to have one and a few spares); a completed tangram square to display towards the end of the lesson; card; scissors; pencils; rulers

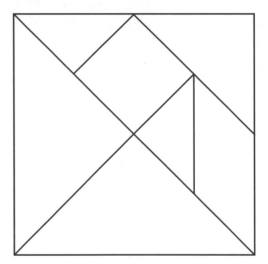

WHAT TO DO

● Look at the shapes in your set.
● Take it in turns to describe each shape to a partner.
● Run your finger around the edge of the shapes to help you remember the corners and direction of the sides.
● Use your shapes to make other shapes and objects.

NOW TRY THIS

1. Make a picture using all of the shapes.
2. Make a square with the shapes. Look at the one on display. Is yours right?
3. Make a picture using two tangrams.
4. Make your own tangram set from card.

TESSELLATING

THINKING SKILL: enquiry
SUBJECT LINK: mathematics
LEARNING LINK: visual
ORGANISATION: small groups, pairs or individuals
RESOURCES: a large number of shapes of different sorts and sizes; large sheets of paper; a digital camera

WHAT TO DO

● Choose any shape and collect about 20 examples of it – they should be the same size.
● Try to fit them together on your paper so that there are no spaces in between.
● Share what you have done with a partner who chose the same shape.
● Have you fitted the shapes together in the same way?
● The patterns you have made are called tessellating patterns.

NOW TRY THIS

1. Use the same shape to make different tessellating patterns.
2. Join the shapes along the whole of one side, diagonally and straight.
3. Join them half way along each side or at the corners.
4. How many different patterns can you make?
5. Find another shape that will tessellate.
6. Find a shape that needs another to tessellate with.
7. Find a shape that won't tessellate. Why not?

ANSWERS
Here are some examples of tessellating patterns.

ALPHABETICAL OBJECTS

THINKING SKILL: information processing
SUBJECT LINK: English (literacy)
LEARNING LINK: visual
ORGANISATION: groups
RESOURCES: floor cards with letters of the alphabet; a set of objects starting with each letter of the alphabet; a set of objects of different textures, materials, colour and other properties that match each letter of the alphabet

WHAT TO DO

● Sort the letters into alphabetical order.
● Get out your objects and arrange them into a group so that you can all see them.
● Take it in turns to choose an object. Match it to the letter label that it starts with. As you pick it, say its name, the phoneme it starts with and the letter label you are matching it to.
● Take it in turns until all of the objects have been matched to a letter label.

NOW TRY THIS

Do this again, but this time match the objects to a different letter using a property rather than the object's name.

TEXTURED SCULPTURES

THINKING SKILL: creative thinking
SUBJECT LINK: art and design
LEARNING LINK: visual
ORGANISATION: groups
RESOURCES: a collection of clean objects with different textures such as feathers, cotton wool, stones, sand, sticks, fabric, bubble wrap, bark, straw, string, wool, paper; card for labels; pens

WHAT TO DO

● Sit in a circle around your collection of materials. For two minutes, discuss words to describe their textures.
● Write the textures on labels.
● Choose one texture and make a class sculpture to represent this.

NOW TRY THIS

1. Your teacher will give you a label.
2. Choose a few materials that match this texture and make a group sculpture.
3. Give your sculpture a name that represents the texture.

LACING UP

THINKING SKILL: information processing
SUBJECT LINK: PE
LEARNING LINK: visual
ORGANISATION: pairs
RESOURCES: pairs of lace-up shoes or trainers or card templates laced in different ways (one pair per pair of children), one shoe laced and the other not; laces

WHAT TO DO

● With your partner, look at how the shoe is laced up.
● Talk together about how it is laced.
● Talk about how the laces go over and under each other.
● Is it laced by going under or over the hole before being threaded through?
● Is the shoe laced in a criss-cross or straight line pattern? Try to lace up the other shoe in the same way.
● Decide whether to start the lacing near the toe or the ankle to leave the ends of the laces for tying in a bow.
● Decide whether to thread the ends from under or over the holes.
● Which hole needs to be threaded next?
● Look at both shoes. Have you threaded the second shoe correctly?

NOW TRY THIS

Swap shoes with another group that has a different threading pattern.

ANSWERS

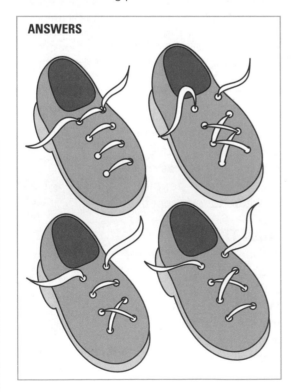

LETTER WALKS

THINKING SKILL: enquiry
SUBJECT LINK: English (handwriting)
LEARNING LINK: visual
ORGANISATION: individuals
RESOURCES: pencil crayons including red, green and orange; A4 sheets of paper; letters of the alphabet worksheet

WHAT TO DO

● Look at the alphabet. Choose a letter that you need to learn how to write correctly.
● Write this letter large on a sheet of paper.
● Decide where the letter starts and put a green dot.
● Decide where the letter finishes and put a red dot.
● Trace over this letter at least ten times, using different colours each time to make a rainbow letter.
● Add your rainbow letters around the edge of the paper to make a border of the same letter.

NOW TRY THIS

1. For each letter on the alphabet worksheet, put a green dot where the letter starts, and a red dot where it finishes.
2. Go over the letters to check if you are correct.
3. If it is a letter with an extra stroke or dot such as **t**, **f**, **i**, **j**, **x** and possibly **k** (depending on how you write this letter), add this in orange.

ANSWERS
The letters can be grouped according to their starting and/or finishing places and the direction they follow when written:

c, o, a, d, g, q *is one group;*
i, l, t, f, j *is another;*
k, b, h, m, n, p, r *is another;*
u *and* **y** *go together, and* **v** *and* **w**;
e, s, x *and* **z** *stand alone.*

BEAD JEWELLERY

THINKING SKILL: information processing
SUBJECT LINK: mathematics
LEARNING LINK: visual
ORGANISATION: whole-class introduction, individual task
RESOURCES: beads of different colours, shapes and sizes; laces

WHAT TO DO

• Watch your teacher threading beads onto a lace, following a pattern.
• What pattern is made? Is your teacher using a sequence of colours or shapes?
• Use two different colours and make a pattern. You can add one of each colour to make your pattern, or two or three of each colour.
• Compare the bead necklaces that everyone has made.

NOW TRY THIS

1. Make a pattern with one of one colour, two of the next and three of the next. Repeat the pattern twice more.
2. Now make a pattern with different-shaped beads – for example, a round bead and then a cylindrical one.
3. Swap with a partner and follow their pattern to finish their necklace.

MOVE IT ABOUT

THINKING SKILL: reasoning
SUBJECT LINK: science
LEARNING LINK: visual
ORGANISATION: small groups
RESOURCES: several different types of tongs and tweezers; magnets; a piece of paper; a collection of objects of different sizes and materials that can be picked up with tongs and tweezers or moved with a magnet

WHAT TO DO

• Look at the objects.
• Sort them by size.
• Which ones can you pick up with the tweezers?
• Which ones do you need to use the tongs to move? Why?
• Are there any objects that you can move without using your hands or the tweezers and tongs? Try this.
• Sort your objects into three sets: those that you can move with tweezers, those with tongs and those with a magnet.

NOW TRY THIS

1. Move all of the objects from your table to the next table without touching them with your hands.
2. How can you get the objects that you need to move with a magnet to the next table? Use a piece of paper to help.
3. Find other objects around the classroom to add to your sets. Remember, you can only use the tweezers, tongs or a magnet.

BLIND SORTING

THINKING SKILL: enquiry
SUBJECT LINK: science
LEARNING LINK: visual, auditory
ORGANISATION: small groups
RESOURCES: for each group: magnets; a collection of objects made from different materials that can be sorted by other means than sight; large sheets of paper; sorting rings and cards for labels (a different assortment of buttons is good to include in this activity). Safety note: be careful when asking the children to use taste to identify objects

WHAT TO DO

• Look at the objects. Talk about and list their properties.
• Look at the list of properties and cross out all those you have named by using your sense of sight (for example, transparency and colour).
• Next to the other properties, say whether you could name the property using your sense of touch, hearing, smell or taste.
• Are some objects in more than one set?

NOW TRY THIS

1. Sort the objects into sets according to their properties, using any sense except sight.
2. Label your sets and say which sense you used to sort them.
3. Walk around the room. How have other groups sorted their objects?

FOLDED LILY

THINKING SKILL: enquiry
SUBJECT LINK: art and design, PSHE
LEARNING LINK: visual
ORGANISATION: individual task within small group
RESOURCES: an adult to support the folding activity; pencils; squares of coloured paper; a print of one of Monet's water lily paintings; a display board with the background to the painting already painted in an art lesson

WHAT TO DO

● Talk about Monet's painting of water lilies.
● Tell the children that they will make some of their own lilies to add to the background on the board.

NOW TRY THIS

1. Find the centre of your paper square by folding it in half and then in half again.
2. Open up the paper square.
3. Fold the four corners into the centre so they meet exactly, creasing the edges
4. You should now have a smaller square.
5. Turn the paper over. Repeat the folding as before.
6. Turn the four corners into the centre so they meet exactly.
7. You should now have an even smaller square.
8. Fold your square in half to make a rectangle.
9. Fold your rectangle in half to make a square.
10. Now comes the difficult bit!
11. Put your forefinger and thumb of your right hand inside two flaps and the forefinger and thumb on your left hand in the other two flaps.
12. Push your folded shape into the shape of a lily.
13. Display your lilies on a large board to create a picture.

UP-LIFTING LILIES

THINKING SKILL: enquiry
SUBJECT LINK: art and design, PSHE
LEARNING LINK: visual
ORGANISATION: individual task within small group
RESOURCES: an adult to help with the folding activity; pencils; folded lilies like those made in previous activity

WHAT TO DO

● Make a folded lily and open it up so that you have the triangular flaps towards you.

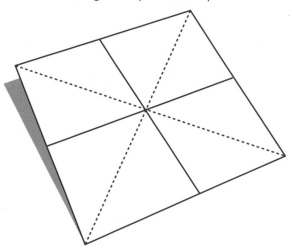

● Write the name of a colour on each of the triangular sections of the lily.
● Underneath each flap, write a short message telling the person choosing the colour that they have a special quality. The message must be positive.
● Play this game with a partner.
● Ask your partner to choose a number.
● Move the lily in the two directions, counting as you do so.
● Finish with the lily open.
● Read the four colours that are showing. Invite your partner to choose one.
● Lift the flap. Read what it says under the colour your partner has chosen.

NOW TRY THIS

Instead of messages, include sums for your friend to work out or questions for them to answer about history or another subject.

DOMINOES

THINKING SKILL: enquiry
SUBJECT LINK: science
LEARNING LINK: visual
ORGANISATION: pairs or small groups
RESOURCES: collections of identical objects with different textures; blank arrow cards for labelling; pencils

WHAT TO DO
● Look at the objects in your collection.
● Sort them into sets, thinking about their textures.
● Give your sets a label.

NOW TRY THIS
1. Take any one object and place it at the edge of the table.
2. Find another object that has the same texture as the first object and place it at the edge but a short distance away from the first object.
3. Write your reason for linking the two objects on an arrow and place this between them.
4. Continue in this way until you have organised objects around the edge of your table in an unbroken circle.
5. Put other objects across the centre of the circle like spokes in a wheel.

STRAW TRIANGLES

THINKING SKILL: creative thinking
SUBJECT LINK: mathematics
LEARNING LINK: visual
ORGANISATION: individuals or pairs
RESOURCES: straws of the same length

WHAT TO DO
● Use the straws to make a triangle.
● Write down how many straws you used.
● Predict how many straws you will need to make two triangles.
● Make the triangles.
● Write down how many straws you used this time. Did you use more or fewer than you thought?

● Did anyone make the two triangles with only five straws? How?

NOW TRY THIS
1. Make two triangles with five straws.
2. Make three triangles with seven straws.
3. Make four triangles with nine straws.
4. Make five triangles with 11 straws.
5. What is the least number of straws needed to make six triangles?

ANSWERS
The least number of straws needed to make 6 triangles is 12 if they are organised as a hexagon.

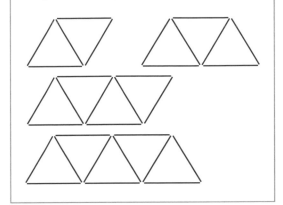

STRIP PENTAGONS

THINKING SKILL: reasoning
SUBJECT LINK: mathematics
LEARNING LINK: visual
ORGANISATION: individuals and pairs
RESOURCES: several sets of identical lengths of Meccano™; split pins; large sheets of paper

WHAT TO DO
● Join the ends of five strips of Meccano™, using the split pins to make a pentagon. The strips must be the same length.
● Move the Meccano™ around to make as many different shapes as you can.
● Draw around the shapes as you make them to keep a record.
● Share your ideas with a partner.
● Has your partner created a shape you haven't?

NOW TRY THIS
1. Use the Meccano™ shape to make a star.
2. Draw round the star when you have succeeded.
3. How many sides and how many corners are there?
4. Show your partner how you made the star.

BRICKWALL

THINKING SKILL: reasoning
SUBJECT LINK: design and technology
LEARNING LINK: visual
ORGANISATION: individuals and pairs
RESOURCES: double and single LEGO™ brick; large bricks

WHAT TO DO

● Make a two-storey wall with LEGO™ that you can pick up without it falling apart.
● What do you have to do with the joins to make sure it doesn't fall apart?
● How many single LEGO™ bricks did you need to use to make each row the same length?
● Add another row of bricks. Is this row the same pattern as the first or second row?
● Add another row of bricks. Which row did you copy?

NOW TRY THIS

1. Use the LEGO™ bricks to make a square shape two bricks high. How did you turn the corner? Did you overlap the bricks?
2. Make a tall tower with large bricks.
3. Make a bridge.

500 GRAMS

THINKING SKILL: reasoning
SUBJECT LINK: mathematics
LEARNING LINK: visual
ORGANISATION: pairs
RESOURCES: balance scales; one 1kg weight; one 500g weight; sand; a container

WHAT TO DO

● Weigh out 1kg of sand in one pan using the 1kg weight.
● How will you know when you have weighed

exactly 1kg of sand?
● Fill the other pan with another 1kg of sand.
● How will you know when you have weighed another 1kg of sand?
● Pour the sand back into its container.
● Weigh out 500g of sand in the same way.
● Remember that 500g is half of a kilogram.

NOW TRY THIS

1. Weigh out 500g of sand using the 1kg weight. How did you do it?
2. If 250g is half of 500g, weigh out 250g using the 500g weight.
3. Weigh out 250g of sand using the 1kg weight.
4. Weigh out 750g of sand. Remember that 750g is 500g plus 250g.
5. Use 1kg and 250g weights to make 500g and 750g.

PAPER BRIDGE

THINKING SKILL: reasoning
SUBJECT LINK: science, design and technology
LEARNING LINK: visual
ORGANISATION: small groups
RESOURCES: sheets of A4 paper; sticky tape; 100g, 200g and 500g weights; materials to make a bridge (card, paper, wood and so on)

WHAT TO DO

● Weigh how heavy the 100g weight is in your hand and make a bridge from card, wood or any other materials you can find to carry its weight.

NOW TRY THIS

1. Make a bridge just from paper to carry the 100g weight.
2. Make a bridge from one sheet of paper to carry the 100g weight. Clue: you may need to fold the paper and/or secure the edges to the side supports with sticky tape.
3. Test out how strong your bridge is.
4. Pretend the 100g, 200g and 500g weights are the Three Billy Goats Gruff. Act out the story with a partner, using your bridge for the three goats to cross.
5. Does your bridge hold the weight of all three goats?

ANSWERS
A concertina fold is the strongest for making a bridge from one sheet of paper.

PARTY HATS

THINKING SKILL: creative thinking, information processing
SUBJECT LINK: design and technology
LEARNING LINK: visual
ORGANISATION: individuals
RESOURCES: tissue paper or newspaper (at least A3 size); sticky tape; (read 'The Quangle Wangle's Hat' from *Laughable Lyrics* by Edward Lear, to go with this activity)

WHAT TO DO

● Make a party hat.
● Fold your paper in half lengthways.

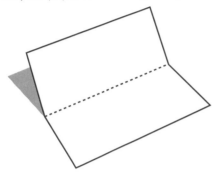

● Fold the top left-hand corner over to the centre to about 10cm from the bottom edge.
● Fold the right top corner over to meet it.

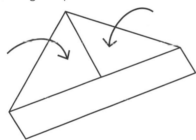

● Fold one bottom edge over the folds to stop them opening up again.
● Fold the other bottom edge backwards behind the hat.

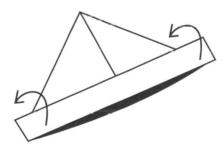

● Open the hat and put it on your head.

NOW TRY THIS

1. Use the paper and sticky tape to make a different-shaped hat.
2. Decorate your hat fit for the Quangle Wangle to wear.

SIX STRAW SHAPES

THINKING SKILL: creative thinking
SUBJECT LINK: mathematics
LEARNING LINK: visual
ORGANISATION: individuals or pairs
RESOURCES: six straws for each child or pair; pipe-cleaners to make corners; scissors

WHAT TO DO

● Use the straws and make as many shapes and pictures as you can. You don't need to use all of the straws to make some of the shapes.
● Share your pictures with your partner.
● How many different shapes and pictures have you made?

NOW TRY THIS

1. Join the straws with the pipe-cleaners to make them secure.
2. Use all six straws to:
   a. make a rectangle
   b. make a triangle
   c. make a hexagon
   d. make a square (you may need to cut one or two straws)
   e. make a pyramid (again, you may need to cut a few straws).

ANSWERS

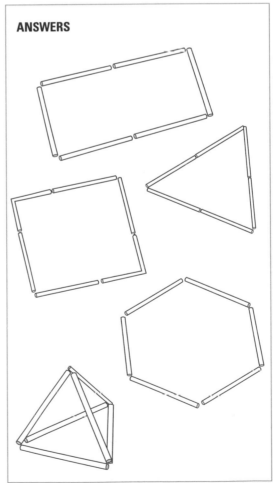

AMAZING MARBLES

THINKING SKILL: reasoning
SUBJECT LINK: science
LEARNING LINK: visual
ORGANISATION: small groups
RESOURCES: Plasticine or Blu-Tack; LEGO™ bricks; board; chalk; marbles

WHAT TO DO

● Roll your marble. In which direction does it go?
● Does it go in a different direction every time you set it off? Why?
● Put your marble on the board and try to get it to roll down in a straight line.
● Were you successful?
● Now draw a pathway on the board with chalk. Can get your marble to follow the pathway?
● How easy was it?

NOW TRY THIS

Use the Plasticine and LEGO™ bricks to make barriers that will guide your marble along the route you have drawn.

FILL IT UP

THINKING SKILL: reasoning
SUBJECT LINK: mathematics
LEARNING LINK: visual
ORGANISATION: pairs and small groups
RESOURCES: water; 1 litre, 500ml and 250ml measures; a bucket or similar container

WHAT TO DO

● Measure out 500ml of water in the litre container. Can you find more than one way to do this?

NOW TRY THIS

1. Measure out 250ml of water in the litre container. Can you find more than one way to do this?

2. Answer these questions:
   a. *How many 250ml in 500ml?*
   b. *How many 250ml in 1 litre?*
   c. *How many 250ml in 750ml?*

MAKE A LANTERN

THINKING SKILL: information processing, enquiry
SUBJECT LINK: design and technology
LEARNING LINK: visual, auditory
ORGANISATION: individuals working in groups
RESOURCES: sheets of A4 and A3 coloured paper (cut the A3 sheets in half along the long side); rulers; pencils; scissors; glue or sticky tape

WHAT TO DO

● Fold your sheet of A4 paper in half lengthways.
● Draw a line about two centimetres from the unfolded edge.
● Cut straight lines about one centimetre apart from the folded edge up to the line you have drawn.
● Open up your paper and join the two shorter edges together, overlapping the edges a bit.
● Stick the edges with glue or sticky tape.
● Make a handle for your lantern.

CHANGE IT AGAIN

THINKING SKILL: information processing, enquiry, evaluation, reasoning
SUBJECT LINK: science
LEARNING LINK: visual, auditory
ORGANISATION: groups
RESOURCES: a set of objects made from a range of materials, some of which can have their shapes changed easily by physical force while others cannot (fabric, foil, paper, card, wool, string, and cotton wool, solid metal, plastic and wood)

WHAT TO DO

- Look at the range of materials.
- Can you change their shape? Sort them into sets of 'Yes' or 'No'.
- Check the materials in the set that you think cannot be changed to make sure.

NOW TRY THIS

1. Decide how many ways you can change the shape of the cotton wool. Try this out. What actions did you take? Did the cotton wool spring back into its original shape?
2. Do the same with the paper, fabric, wool, string and card. Notice that all these materials are flexible and can be folded, twisted and plaited.
3. Now look at the foil together. This is a metal material. How is it different from the other metal objects in your set? What properties does the foil have that the others do not?

FEEL THE SHAPE

THINKING SKILL: reasoning, enquiry
SUBJECT LINK: mathematics
LEARNING LINK: visual
ORGANISATION: groups
RESOURCES: Logiblocs™; drawstring bags; sorting rings; labels (A4 paper with titles will do). Each group will need half a box of Logiblocs™, separated into shapes (one group will have the circles and rectangles and another the squares and triangles, and so on). On each label write the attributes of all the shapes in the box except the colour – for example, large thick circles or small thin squares

WHAT TO DO

- Look at your shapes. What do you notice about their size and thickness?
- Sort the shapes into sets according to their size.

- Now sort them according to their thickness and then their shape names.

NOW TRY THIS

1. Place all of the shapes inside your drawstring bag. Spread the labels around your table.
2. Take it in turns to feel inside the bag to find a shape. Before taking the shape from the bag, pick up its matching label. Put the label and shape together on the table.
3. Why are there no labels to sort the shapes by colour?

HANG UP THE WASHING

THINKING SKILL: reasoning
SUBJECT LINK: mathematics
LEARNING LINK: visual
ORGANISATION: whole class or groups
RESOURCES: washing lines hung across a display board, between two chairs, or across the corner of a room (one line per group); a set of clothing for each group; enough pegs to hang up all the items; paper; pencils; a list of clothing and the number of pegs needed to hang them (see below)

> Sock = one peg
> handkerchief = two pegs
> underpants = two pegs
> towel = three pegs
> vest or T-shirt = two pegs
> trousers or skirt = two pegs

WHAT TO DO

- Look at the items of clothing that have been collected. Look at the list shown above, and decide how many pegs you need altogether to hang up the washing on the line.
- Hang the washing on the line. Count the number of pegs. Were you right?
- Can you hang out the washing with fewer pegs?

NOW TRY THIS

Work out the least number of pegs you will need to hang up six handkerchiefs if two handkerchiefs can be hung up with three pegs.

> **ANSWERS**
> You will need two pegs for one handkerchief, three for two handkerchiefs, four for three and so on. You will need seven pegs to hang up six handkerchiefs.

HEAVY AND LIGHT

THINKING SKILL: enquiry, reasoning
SUBJECT LINK: mathematics
LEARNING LINK: visual
ORGANISATION: groups
RESOURCES: several containers of different shapes and sizes with different amounts of dry sand or water so that they weigh different masses (groups should be given either sand or water containers); bottles and containers with lids; dry sand; water; empty containers; plastic sheeting (label all of the cartons in each group with numbers)

WHAT TO DO

● Pass the parcels or bottles around so that you can all feel how heavy they are.
● Decide which is the heaviest and lightest.
● Now place the other parcels or bottles in the right order according to how heavy or light they are. Number the order, from lightest to heaviest. Write on your sheet whether you are testing water or sand.
● If you are testing sand, pair up with a group testing the water bottles and vice versa.
● Check each other's answers.

NOW TRY THIS

1. Work in your group to find out which is the heaviest – water or sand.
2. Do you think sand or water is the heaviest?
3. Next check with an adult what you will need.
4. Fill two identical containers, one with water and one with sand. Pass the containers around the group. Do you all agree which weighs more?

CONCERTINA CHAINS

THINKING SKILL: reasoning, creative thinking
SUBJECT LINK: design and technology
LEARNING LINK: auditory
ORGANISATION: individuals
RESOURCES: several sheets of A4 paper cut in half lengthways; pencils, crayons or felt-tipped pens; scissors

WHAT TO DO

● Fold your paper in half lengthways and cut out a shape.

● Open your paper. What pattern have you made?
● Now fold your paper in a concertina way. Cut out a shape (making sure the shape goes to the edge of the paper), open your paper and see what you have made.
● Try to cut out the shape of a Christmas tree or butterfly.

NOW TRY THIS

1. Fold another piece of paper in a concertina lengthways. Cut out the shape of a heart on the edges. Open your paper and see if the holes are in the shape of a heart.
2. Fold your paper in a concertina and cut out a heart shape, but this time make sure you go to the edge of the paper with your cuts like the one in the illustration below. Open your paper. What do you notice now? You should see a row of paper hearts.

WHAT'S IN THE SOCK?

THINKING SKILL: information processing, reasoning
SUBJECT LINK: science
LEARNING LINK: visual
ORGANISATION: individuals
RESOURCES: one sock for each child; an object that is safe to touch inside each sock and a matching object in a different sock on another table in the classroom

WHAT TO DO

● Put your hand inside the sock. Feel the texture, shape and size of the object.
● Without removing the object, move around the classroom until you think you have found its matching partner.
● Check whether you are right.
● Put one object back inside the sock and swap socks with a classmate.

NOW TRY THIS

Find as many partner objects as you can in seven minutes.

DESIGN A BEACH TOWEL

THINKING SKILL: creative thinking, evaluation
SUBJECT LINK: design and technology
LEARNING LINK: visual
ORGANISATION: whole-class introduction, then groups
RESOURCES: large sheets of paper; felt-tipped pens; A4 sheets of paper; pencils and crayons; seaside pictures; a few novelty towels (including some beach towels)

WHAT TO DO

● Spend two minutes looking at the novelty towels. Decide which ones would be suitable for a beach towel. Do you like the way it looks? Do you like the way it feels?
● What sort of motifs would be suitable for a beach towel. Why?

NOW TRY THIS

1. As a group, share your ideas about motifs to include in your designs.
2. Take it in turns to draw them.

3. On your own, design your beach towel. Think before you start. What motifs will you use? What size and position will they have? Which one will be the main motif? Which will be less important and smaller?
4. Sketch your designs. Put them in the place you have decided. (They do not need to be perfect at this stage.)
5. Label your design with the name of the motif and the colours you intend to use.

SYMMETRY

THINKING SKILL: information processing
SUBJECT LINK: mathematics
LEARNING LINK: visual
ORGANISATION: individuals or pairs
RESOURCES: symmetrical card or plastic templates large enough for the children to feel around the edge – mathematics sorting resources are a useful source for these but also Christmas trees, stars, shapes, hearts and butterflies; A3-size sheets of paper; felt-tipped pens

WHAT TO DO

● Choose one of the symmetrical templates and place it in front of you.
● Put the forefingers of both hands at the top centre of the template. Feel around the edge with both fingers moving together in opposite directions until they meet at the bottom.
● Do this again with another template.
● Now try it with your eyes closed.
● Did your fingers still meet at the bottom?

NOW TRY THIS

1. Place a sheet of paper in front of you. Place both fingers together at the top of the paper, close your eyes and draw a triangle by moving both fingers at the same time in opposite directions until they meet at the bottom.
2. Now try it again, but this time draw a square.
3. What about a Christmas tree?
4. Pick up two felt-tipped pens and draw symmetrical pictures, shapes and patterns with both hands at the same time. Try it with your eyes closed.

KINAESTHETIC LEARNING

NOW TRY THIS

1. Try moving backward one unit, then moving backward one ten.

2. Move forward one unit, one ten, one unit, one ten, move backward one unit, one ten, one unit and one ten and so on.

ADDING BIG NUMBERS

THINKING SKILL: reasoning, evaluation
SUBJECT LINK: mathematics
LEARNING LINK: visual, auditory
ORGANISATION: small groups
RESOURCES: a 100-square large enough for the children to walk the numbers; clipboards and pens

WHAT TO DO

● One of you stands on any digit on the 100-square. Take it in turns to direct your friends. Tell them to move forwards or backwards in units or tens.

NOW TRY THIS

1. Write down 24 and 52.

2. Now think of a way to calculate the total.

3. Stand on the number 24. Think how many tens and units are in 52 (5 tens and 2 units). Then move forward 52 squares by moving forward the right number of units and then tens. (Move forward 2 units, then up 5 rows.)

4. Are you standing on 76?

5. Now do the calculation again. This time stand on 24 and move forward the number of tens and then units. (Move up 5 rows, and then forward 2 units.)

6. Are you standing on 76?

7. This time calculate the total by finding and standing on 52 and moving forward 24.

8. Are you standing on 76?

9. Which way was easiest?

ONES AND TENS

THINKING SKILL: reasoning
SUBJECT LINK: mathematics
LEARNING LINK: auditory, visual
ORGANISATION: whole class or groups
RESOURCES: a 100-square large enough for the children to walk the numbers; clipboards and pens; an adult to introduce the games

WHAT TO DO

● Assign a different digit to each of the children. When you call out their number, they find and stand on the correct digit in the 100-square.

● Ask them to stand on a number that has a unit digit less than six.

● Call out instructions to move forwards and backwards by one unit, and then by ten.

● Each time they move, the children should write down the new number, and how many units or tens they moved. Which way did they need to move? What do they notice about the numbers?

● The children should learn that they need to move to the right to move forward by a unit, and that the quickest way to move ten units is to move one row up or down, rather than along ten squares. When they move one unit, the unit digit changes but when they move in tens the ten digit changes.

SNAKES AND LADDERS

THINKING SKILL: reasoning
SUBJECT LINK: mathematics
LEARNING LINK: visual
ORGANISATION: small groups
RESOURCES: a 100-square large enough for the children to walk the numbers; card ladders and paper or fabric snakes; a large dice or spinner

WHAT TO DO

● Place the snakes and ladders on the grid.
● Play the game with your friends.
● Throw the dice and move forward the right number of squares going up the ladders or down the snakes.

NOW TRY THIS

1. Use two dice so that you have to calculate the total before moving.
2. Add a ten digit to each number so that if you throw a 6 you move 16, and so on.

FROM HERE TO THERE

THINKING SKILL: enquiry, evaluation
SUBJECT LINK: ICT, English (speaking and listening), mathematics
LEARNING LINK: visual
ORGANISATION: pairs
RESOURCES: sheets of paper; pencils

WHAT TO DO

● With a friend, decide on a place you would like to go, within the school environment.
● Write down the instructions for getting to this place. Remember to make the instructions precise, such as: *Turn left at the boys' toilets*.
● Follow your instructions. Are they clear enough? Do you need to add more to make them easier to follow?

NOW TRY THIS

1. Swap your directions with another pair.
2. Follow their instructions. Where do you end up?

3. Discuss with the other pair whether their instructions were easy to follow.
4. What did they think of your instructions?
5. Improve the instructions. Swap with another pair to see if they are better.

RIGHT AND LEFT

THINKING SKILL: information processing
SUBJECT LINK: PE
LEARNING LINK: auditory
ORGANISATION: whole class
RESOURCES: a piece of music with a steady 32 beats, such as *In Dulce Jubilo* by Mike Oldfield; an adult to teach the sequences and call out *right* and *left* as the children dance (facing the same way as the children so that they can copy)

WHAT TO DO

● Listen to the music and clap along with the beat.
● Identify when the tune starts again.
● Count the number of claps before the tune starts again – there are 32 beats or claps.

NOW TRY THIS

1. Learn this right/left dance.
2. Pat your right hand on your right thigh for four beats and then your left hand on your left thigh for four beats.
3. Do this sequence four times until the tune starts again.
4. Now stamp your right foot four times and then your left foot four times.
5. Do this sequence four times until the tune starts again.
6. Now put the two sequences together. Stamp your right foot at the same time as patting your right thigh with your hand four times, and then the same for the left hand and foot.
7. Repeat this sequence four times.
8. Next push your right arm up to the sky four times and then your left arm four times.
9. Repeat this sequence four times.
10. Make four side steps to the right and then four to the left.
11. Repeat this sequence four times.
12. Repeat the side-step sequence and add the arm movement (steps 8–9) as you move to the right and then left.
13. Now do the dance sequence saying *right* when you are using your right hand, arm or foot, or moving to the right, and saying *left* when you are using your left hand, arm or foot, or moving to the left.

SQUARE DANCE

THINKING SKILL: information processing
SUBJECT LINK: PE
LEARNING LINK: auditory
ORGANISATION: whole class
RESOURCES: a piece of music with a steady 32 beats, such as *In Dulce Jubilo* by Mike Oldfield; an adult to supervise and direct the dance (give each pair a number – 1, 2, 3 and 4)

WHAT TO DO

● Get into groups of eight and stand with a partner in a square formation.

● Hold hands and dance in a circle to the right, saying *right* in time to your steps and the music as you do so, for 16 beats.
● Now dance to the left, saying *left* in time to your steps and the music as you do so, for 16 beats.
● Point to your opposite partners with your right hand for four beats and then with your left, saying *right* and *left* as appropriate.
● Do this four times.
● Pair numbers 1 and 3 cross over places, shaking their opposite number's right hand (this should be done in eight beats).
● Next, pair numbers 2 and 4 cross over to the next eight beats, passing on the right.
● Copy the sequence, returning to your places.
● Now do this cross-over sequence again, but this time shake left hands and pass each other on the left-hand side.

NOW TRY THIS

1. Face your partner. Cross places with them on the right-hand side, shaking hands as you do so. You should now be facing another partner.
2. Cross over this new partner on the left side, shaking left hands as you do so.

3. You should now be facing your first partner again. Cross over on the right side again.
4. You should now be facing your second partner. Cross over on the left side.
5. Repeat the dance but this time call out *right* and *left* as you move to the right and left.

SEATING PLAN

THINKING SKILL: reasoning
SUBJECT LINK: mathematics
LEARNING LINK: visual
ORGANISATION: groups of three of four children
RESOURCES: one set of grids for each group – 3×3, 4×4 and 5×5; small toys or counters

WHAT TO DO

● Place the toys on the 3×3 grid so that there are at least two, but never three, in each row and column.
● Place the toys on the 4×4 grid so that there are always three, but never four, in each row and column. Can you do this so that there are never more than three in each diagonal too?
● Who succeeded and how did you do it? Who can see a pattern? How many ways did your group find?

NOW TRY THIS

Try it with a 5×5 grid. This time there must be at least four, and never five, in each row, column and diagonal.

ANSWERS

3 × 3

X	X	
X		X
	X	X

4 × 4

X		X	X
X	X	X	
X	X		X
	X	X	X

or

X	X	X	
X		X	X
	X	X	X
X	X		X

5 × 5

X		X	X	X
X	X	X	X	
X	X		X	X
	X	X	X	X
X	X	X		X

POINTING FINGERS

THINKING SKILL: enquiry, creative thinking
SUBJECT LINK: music, science
LEARNING LINK: visual, auditory
ORGANISATION: whole class
RESOURCES: a copy of 'Put your finger on your head' by Woody Guthrie from *Okki-Tokki-Unga: Action Songs for Children* (A&C Black)

WHAT TO DO

● Learn the tune by singing through the first verse.
● Now sing the song again, but this time with your eyes closed.
● Now try these words with these actions to make it harder:

With your left hand hold your nose, hold your nose,
With your right hand hold your ear on the left,
Swap them over, swap them over,
Swap them over, swap them over,
Swap them over, swap them over, do your best.

NOW TRY THIS

1. Now make up some actions of your own.
2. Try standing on your right foot and touching your left hip or knee with your right hand and then swapping them over.

LEARN TO SKIP

THINKING SKILL: information processing
SUBJECT LINK: PE
LEARNING LINK: visual
ORGANISATION: whole class
RESOURCES: a large space

WHAT TO DO

● March around the space. Keep a steady pace.
● Next hop on one foot and then on the other.
● Hop twice on one foot and then twice on the other.

NOW TRY THIS

1. Step forward one step and add a little hop afterwards. Step forward another step and add a little hop on this foot.
2. As you move say *step hop, step hop,* changing feet after every time you say *hop.*
3. Speed up and you will find yourself skipping.
4. Practise skipping to music.

SKIP WITH A ROPE

THINKING SKILL: information processing
SUBJECT LINK: PE
LEARNING LINK: auditory
ORGANISATION: individuals
RESOURCES: skipping ropes; a large space

WHAT TO DO

● Stand in a space and with your arms outstretched. Move them in a circle in a forward direction from the shoulders.
● If you are not sure, watch an adult or a friend.
● Now do this and walk around at the same time.

NOW TRY THIS

1. Find a skipping rope.
2. Make your rope the right length by holding it in outstretched arms.
3. Move your outstretched arms around in a circle in a forward direction, in the same way as you did when you were not holding a rope.
4. As the rope lands on the ground, step over it.
5. Repeat the shoulder movement. Make sure you keep your arms outstretched.
6. Walk around the space, stepping over the rope every time it lands on the floor in front of your feet.
7. Try to do this a little faster.
8. Then instead of walking, run slowly.
9. If you get the rope caught in your feet, go back to walking until you are ready to run.

SEQUENCE DANCING

THINKING SKILL: information processing
SUBJECT LINK: music
LEARNING LINK: visual, auditory
ORGANISATION: whole class and small groups
RESOURCES: a copy of a conga tune and something to play it on (for example, a tape recorder or CD player)

WHAT TO DO

● Listen carefully to the tune. Once you are familiar with the tempo, join in by marching along.
● Listen again. Change the actions so that you are stepping twice and clapping twice.
● Now listen to the tune once more. This time, step twice and jump twice.

NOW TRY THIS

1. Work with a partner.
2. One of you is the leader. Make up a set of actions for your friend to copy.
3. Swap over.
4. As you listen to the song again, first add your actions and then your friend's actions.
5. Join with another pair and put the sequences together.

WALK THE SHAPE

THINKING SKILL: information processing, reasoning
SUBJECT LINK: mathematics
LEARNING LINK: auditory, visual
ORGANISATION: whole class
RESOURCES: a safe space for the children to work outside; 2-D shapes; chalk

WHAT TO DO

● Hold up the shapes in turn. Ask the children to find a shape that matches it, either on the ground, fences or walls around them. Make sure they find a different object each time the same shape is held up.
● Group the children into pairs. Draw a large circle on the ground. One child from each pair walks around the circle.
● Tell them to describe to their partner what they just did. They should think about what they did *not* do as well. For example, they did not make any sharp turns, turn a corner or walk in a straight line – but they *did* walk on a curved line and finished where they started.

NOW TRY THIS

1. Draw a large square or rectangle. Ask the other child in each pair to walk around it. Ask them to tell their partner what they did and did not do.
2. They should think about how long the lines were on the square and rectangle. How does this help them to remember which shape is which?
3. Encourage the children to remember to describe whether the edges on the shape are straight or not straight, how long the edges are, whether they made a turn or not and how many turns they made.

MAKE THE SHAPE

THINKING SKILL: information processing
SUBJECT LINK: mathematics
LEARNING LINK: visual
ORGANISATION: groups of about eight
RESOURCES: a space for the children to work; 2-D shapes; a digital camera

WHAT TO DO

● Look at the shape of a circle.
● Make a circle shape with your group by holding hands.
● Make sure you are standing in a circle and not an oval shape.
● Now make your shape into an oval.

NOW TRY THIS

1. Make a triangle with the children in your group. How many groups will you need to divide into? Who will stand at each corner? Which way will you face?
2. Make a rectangle in your group by holding hands. You need to make two longer and two shorter edges.
3. Turn your rectangle into a square.
4. What did you do to change into a square?
5. Think of other shapes you could make, such as a rhombus, or a trapezium.
6. Ask an adult to take photographs of your shapes.

ROAMER TRAILS

THINKING SKILL: enquiry, reasoning
SUBJECT LINK: mathematics, ICT, geography
LEARNING LINK: visual
ORGANISATION: groups
RESOURCES: a large space to move about; beanbags; chalk; a Roamer

WHAT TO DO
- Move in a straight line forwards.
- Move in a straight line backwards.
- Move in a diagonal line.
- Are there other ways to move in a straight line?
- Put four beanbags a short distance away from each other in a quadrilateral shape.
- Stand at one beanbag. Try to move from one to the other just moving forwards, backwards or in a diagonal line – no turning is allowed, you have to face the same direction at all times.
- Can this be done? Do you need to turn?
- Put in a turn. Is it easier to move from one beanbag to the other now?

NOW TRY THIS
1. Draw a square on the ground (make the length of the sides equal to three or four Roamer lengths). Stand at one corner and walk the shape by walking forwards and making 90° turns at each corner.
2. Sit in a circle around one person's square.
3. Your teacher will show you how to program the Roamer to walk the shape using the same directions. What number do you need to match the distance on the square?
4. Were you successful?
5. Draw three steps on the ground. Start at the top and walk the steps.
6. Stand or sit in a circle around one person's steps.
7. Program the Roamer to walk the steps.

CLAP, CLICK AND STAMP

THINKING SKILL: reasoning, creative thinking
SUBJECT LINK: music, PE
LEARNING LINK: visual, auditory
ORGANISATION: whole class
RESOURCES: a copy of 'Clap, stamp, slap, click' by Jan Holdstock in *Flying a Round: 88 Rounds and Partner Songs* (A&C Black)

WHAT TO DO
- Learn the song, adding the actions. Click your fingers to the first line, stamp your feet to the second, slap your knees to the third line and clap on the last.

NOW TRY THIS
1. Add levels to your actions.
2. Click your fingers up high to the first verse.
3. Stamp your feet with your arms crossed or swinging to the sides.
4. Slap your knees, bending quite low
5. Clap your hands standing up.
6. Practise this a few times to get it right.
7. Make up another verse. For example:
   Wave your arms above your head,
   Then you touch your toes,
   Both feet jump up and down,
   Clap on the beat.

THE GRAND OLD DUKE

THINKING SKILL: creative thinking
SUBJECT LINK: music, PE
LEARNING LINK: visual, auditory
ORGANISATION: whole class
RESOURCES: a large space

WHAT TO DO
- Sing the song 'The Grand Old Duke of York' through once, putting in the actions – start low and get taller as you march to the top of the hill, and get smaller as you march down.

NOW TRY THIS
Add other verses with appropriate actions as you are marching up and down. For example:
   They clapped their hands
   to the top of the hill and
   they waved them down
   again;
   They waved their arms…
   They stamped their
   feet…

RIGHT AND LEFT SIDES

THINKING SKILL: information processing, reasoning
SUBJECT LINK: music, PE
LEARNING LINK: visual
ORGANISATION: whole class
RESOURCES: a large space

WHAT TO DO

● Stand in a long line across the hall or playground.
● Wave your right hand in the air.
● Wiggle your right foot in front of you.
● Now wave your right hand and wiggle your right foot at the same time.
● Now wave your left hand.
● Wiggle your left foot.
● Wave your left hand and wiggle your left foot at the same time.

NOW TRY THIS

1. Sing the actions to the tune of 'Looby Loo', putting in the actions as you sing. For example:

Wave your right arm in the air, wiggle your right foot too,
Wave your right hand in the air and turn to the right as you do.
Wave your left arm in the air, wiggle your left foot too,
Wave your left hand in the air and turn to the left as you do.

2. Make up verses to add other actions. For example, wiggle your bottom, wiggle your right leg and left leg, shake your body and wave your right arm, shake your body and shake your left arm.

LETTER ACTIONS

THINKING SKILL: creative thinking
SUBJECT LINK: English (literacy)
LEARNING LINK: visual
ORGANISATION: small groups or pairs
RESOURCES: large sheets of paper; A4 paper; pens

WHAT TO DO

● Listen to the sound made from the letter **h**.
● What are you doing to make this sound?
● Put your hand in front of your mouth and feel the heat from this sound. Say *hot hand* as you make this sound.
● Now play a paper chase using a **p** sound.

● Put a sheet of A4 paper on the edge of a table. Have a race with your friend to see who can get the paper to the other end of the table first, using a **p** sound.

NOW TRY THIS

1. Now look at the other letters in the alphabet. Either make sound actions to help you to remember the sound the letters make, or draw clues to help.
2. Draw the letters you have chosen on the large sheet of paper. Either add the visual clue or write a short description of the action.

COORDINATES

THINKING SKILL: reasoning
SUBJECT LINK: geography
LEARNING LINK: auditory, visual
ORGANISATION: whole class organised into groups of six or seven children
RESOURCES: for each group, a small area of ground divided into 16 squares (skipping ropes are good for this); enough toys for every child to have a toy to place; labels with A, B, C, D and 1, 2, 3, 4 written on; a different set of coordinates for each grid

WHAT TO DO

● With the class, look at the way the area has been divided into squares.
● Invite a child to place a toy in one of the squares.
● Ask the class to describe the square the toy is in.
● Invite another child to follow the description to get to the toy.
● Next label the squares A, B, C, D along the bottom and 1, 2, 3, 4 up the left-hand side.
● Ask the children to say which column the toy is in and then which row it is in.
● Does this make it easier to describe the position?

NOW TRY THIS

1. Put the children into groups and assign a grid to each group.
2. Give each child a coordinate. Ask them to put the toys in the correct square.

SONG AND STORY MIME

THINKING SKILL: creative thinking, reasoning
SUBJECT LINK: music, English (speaking and listening)
LEARNING LINK: visual
ORGANISATION: whole class and groups
RESOURCES: none

WHAT TO DO

● Choose a story that the children know but have not listened to for a while. Mime actions from the story. Ask the children to guess which story it is.
● Identify all the songs and stories they know as a class.
● Invite a child to come to the front and mime actions for one of these for the rest of the class to guess.

NOW TRY THIS

1. Organise the children into groups. Invite each group to work out a group mime for a favourite story or song. They should not take up too much time choosing it!
2. In turn, let each group act out their mime for the rest of the class to guess.

SORTING FEATURES

THINKING SKILL: enquiry
SUBJECT LINK: mathematics, science
LEARNING LINK: visual, auditory
ORGANISATION: whole class and then two smaller groups
RESOURCES: set rings and Carroll diagrams chalked on the floor, large enough for the children to stand in; labels for the sorting criteria

WHAT TO DO

● Sort yourselves into sets of children with the same eye colour.
● Now sort yourself into sets with the same hair colour.
● Look at the children in your class and decide other features you could use to sort yourselves into sets, such as children who wear glasses, and those who do not.

NOW TRY THIS

1. Divide into two smaller groups.
2. Label your Carroll diagram *red hair/not red hair* over the top of your columns and *blue eyes/not blue eyes* at the side. Sort yourselves according to the criteria, standing in the matching square.
3. For example, if you have red hair and blue eyes you need to be in the top left-hand square.
4. Answer these questions:
   a. How many children have red hair and blue eyes?
   b. How many children have neither red hair nor blue eyes?
   c. Do all the children with red hair have blue eyes?
   d. Do all the children with a different colour hair have blue eyes?

	Red hair	Not red hair
Blue eyes		
Not blue eyes		

MOVE IT

THINKING SKILL: reasoning, creative thinking, evaluation
SUBJECT LINK: PSHE
LEARNING LINK: tactile
ORGANISATION: small groups
RESOURCES: sand; water; containers; paper; pencils

WHAT TO DO

● Talk together as a group about how you could move a pile of sand from one side of the classroom to the other without touching it. You can use anything you like to help.
● Record your ideas on paper.
● Choose one idea. Write a plan to show how you would work together to move the sand.

NOW TRY THIS

1. Test out your plan.
2. Try two more ideas.
3. Which were the best, and why?
4. Repeat, but now transport water. Could you use the same method as you did for the sand?

EVERYBODY DO THIS

THINKING SKILL: information processing, creative thinking

SUBJECT LINK: English (speaking and listening)

LEARNING LINK: visual, auditory

ORGANISATION: whole class

RESOURCES: A copy of the song 'Everybody do this' by Mary Miller (set to a traditional American folk tune) from *Okki-Tokki-Unga: Action Songs for Children* (A&C Black)

WHAT TO DO

● Teach the song to the children, putting in simple actions such as clapping, clicking fingers, stamping feet and so on.

● Now sing the song again. This time put in two actions at the same time.

NOW TRY THIS

1. Now put in some silly actions, such as tapping your nose and rubbing your knee at the same time, for the children to copy.

2. Ask them to work in small groups or pairs to think of other silly actions for the class to copy.

FIND THE TREASURE

THINKING SKILL: reasoning

SUBJECT LINK: geography, mathematics

LEARNING LINK: visual, auditory

ORGANISATION: whole class organised into an even number of teams (four or six)

RESOURCES: at least three pieces of paper divided into 8x8 squares; three floor spaces divided into 8x8 squares, either made by drawing on the floor or using skipping ropes (label the grid A to H along the bottom and 1 to 8 up the left-hand side); 64 circles, 5 with the letter T written on for treasure (make sure it doesn't show through the paper); pencils

WHAT TO DO

● Team 1 takes it in turn to name a coordinate for each member of Team 2 to find. The member of Team 2 then stands in the matching square.

● Team 2 then does the same for Team 1.

● Check to make sure each person is going to the right square.

NOW TRY THIS

1. Team 1: Choose where to hide your treasure on the grid. Place circles in every square, turning the five circles with treasure on upside down

so the other team cannot see.

2. Team 2: Name a square to try to find where Team 1 has hidden their treasure.

3. Team 1: Turn over the circle chosen by Team 2 to see whether they have found treasure.

4. Team 2: Name another square.

5. Team 1: Check to see if they have found any treasure.

6. Continue until all of the treasure has been found.

7. Swap over. Team 2 is now hiding and Team 1 finding the treasure.

CROOKED AND TWISTED

THINKING SKILL: reasoning

SUBJECT LINK: English (speaking and listening)

LEARNING LINK: auditory

ORGANISATION: whole class

RESOURCES: a large space; a copy of the traditional rhyme 'There was a crooked man'; sheets of paper; pencils

WHAT TO DO

● Recite the rhyme 'There was a crooked man' to the children. Ask them what they think *crooked* means in this rhyme.

● Investigate what was meant by *a crooked man* by asking the children to portray this with their bodies.

● Next investigate what was meant by *walked a crooked mile*. Ask the children to show how the man may walk in a crooked way.

● Explore the meaning of the word *crooked* and recall words and phrases such as *not in a straight line, askew, not upright*.

● Discuss the difference between *crooked* and *wiggly*. Walk in a crooked way and then in a wiggly way. What is the difference?

NOW TRY THIS

On a sheet of paper, draw pictures of crooked items such as a crooked stile, a crooked hat, a crooked walking stick, and a crooked path.

BODY LETTERS

THINKING SKILL: creative thinking
SUBJECT LINK: English (literacy)
LEARNING LINK: visual, auditory
ORGANISATION: groups of three or four, depending on your class's age and ability
RESOURCES: a list of possible letter shapes such as those in the illustration below; you need to know the tune of 'Bingo'

WHAT TO DO

● Sing the song 'Bingo' so the children can learn the tune. Give the dog the name Tommy:

> There was a farmer who had a dog,
> And Tommy was his name-o.
> T-O-M-M-Y
> T-O-M-M-Y
> T-O-M-M-Y
> And Tommy was his name-o.

● Sing it through a second time. This time, do the actions for the letters TOMMY as you sing. Invite the children to copy.
● Use letter actions to spell out other names such as Tammy, Bobby and Poppy (names with five letters and two syllables fit the best).

NOW TRY THIS

1. In your groups, make up other letter shapes with your arms and body.
2. Use the shapes you have made to spell out other names for the dog.
3. Take it in turns to spell out a word for the other groups to work out. This will help you to see how good your body letters were.

A STANDING GRAPH

THINKING SKILL: enquiry
SUBJECT LINK: mathematics
LEARNING LINK: visual
ORGANISATION: whole class and then two smaller groups
RESOURCES: a block and/or bar chart drawn on the floor with the upright axis numbered 1 to at least 10 and the horizontal axis numbered with the shoe sizes the children in your class wear (including half sizes); a second space for a bar chart to record the children's bedtimes

WHAT TO DO

● Check what size shoes you are wearing.
● Stand in the matching column for your size shoe on the block/bar graph.
● Now answer these questions:
    a. How many children wear size 13 shoes?
    b. How many children wear size 10½ shoes?
    c. How many more children wear size 13 than size 10½ shoes?
    d. What is the most frequent shoe size?
    e. What is the least frequent shoe size?
    f. Who has the smallest feet?
    g. Who has the largest feet?
    h. Would you be able to answer the last two questions if you had been drawing a bar chart on paper?
    i. Why not?

NOW TRY THIS

1. Divide into two smaller groups.
2. Find out what time everybody goes to bed.
3. Decide how you could show this on a graph.
4. Draw out a 10x10 grid.
5. Number up the left-hand side (the vertical axis) with numbers 1 to 10.
6. Under each square along the bottom (the horizontal axis) write the times at 15-minute intervals that your group members go to bed. Start with the earliest time at the far left and the latest time on the far right. For example, if the earliest time is 6.00pm the next time you would write is 6.15pm, then 6.30pm, and so on, until you write the latest time.
7. Make a graph to show what time the children in your group go to bed.

KINAESTHETIC LEARNING

UNDERSTANDING MOTION

THINKING SKILL: information processing, creative thinking
SUBJECT LINK: English (speaking and listening)
LEARNING LINK: auditory
ORGANISATION: whole class
RESOURCES: a large space in which to move

WHAT TO DO

● Go into the hall and ask the children to move in different ways. Identify as many different ways of moving as you can.
● Add adverbs to the movements to extend the range, such as skipping slowly or crawling fast.
● Make short phrases to describe the movement more clearly, such as hopping from one foot to the other or running in a spiral.
● Stand the children in a row at the back of the hall. Invite them to move to the front in a different way to the previous person each time. Ask them to describe their movements at the same time. Plan for higher attainers to be last.

NOW TRY THIS

1. Explore different ways of walking such as striding, ambling, marching, dawdling, strolling, to extend the children's vocabulary. Do the same for the different ways of running.
2. Extend the activity by making shapes and movements for words that start with a particular letter string you want the children to learn, such as strong, struggle, stride, stroke, striker; spring, sprightly, spread, spray; or twist, twirl, twelve, twice. Start with the children making a list of words in the classroom before turning them into movements in the hall.

BIGGER OR SMALLER?

THINKING SKILL: reasoning
SUBJECT LINK: mathematics
LEARNING LINK: auditory
ORGANISATION: whole class or small groups
RESOURCES: none required

WHAT TO DO

● Stoop down very low. As you count from 1 to 10, slowly grow taller.
● Count back down to zero, slowly getting lower as you count.

● Do this again but this time count forwards and backwards in twos.
● Take it in turns to call out a number between 1 and 20.
● If the number called is higher than the last one, then the rest of the group should go higher, if lower they should go lower.

NOW TRY THIS

1. Repeat the game for numbers between 1 and 50 and then 1 and 100.
2. Choose a times table you are learning.
3. Take it in turns to ask a question – for example, *What is 5 x 4?*
4. The rest of the group should move higher or lower for the answer, depending on whether the answer is higher or lower than the last answer, saying the answer out loud as they move.

WHAT AM I?

THINKING SKILL: enquiry
SUBJECT LINK: geography, history
LEARNING LINK: visual
ORGANISATION: whole class (this is a useful activity to find out what the children know either at the beginning of the year to inform planning or at the end of the year to find out what they have learned)
RESOURCES: a collection of hats and props to act as clues

WHAT TO DO

● List all the people that the children have learned something about in the previous 12 months. This could include someone visiting the class to talk about their job, a character or famous person from history, or people who work in the local area or further afield.
● Choose someone and act out what that person does for a living and their personality traits, displayed in the way they stand and move.
● Ask the children to guess the person and what they are doing.
● If the children are unable to guess, give them a clue by showing them a prop or giving a verbal clue.

NOW TRY THIS

1. Ask the children to work in groups to create a mime of a person and their job for the rest of the class to guess.
2. Perform each group mime. If the others cannot guess, give them a clue to help them.

MARCHING NUMBERS

THINKING SKILL: information processing, reasoning
SUBJECT LINK: mathematics
LEARNING LINK: auditory
ORGANISATION: whole class (organise the children into groups according to ability for the extension. This way some can practise tens and fives, while others can practise twos, threes and fours)
RESOURCES: a number line visible to the children, from 0 to 50 or 0 to 100, depending on ability

WHAT TO DO

● Count in fives from 0 to 50 or 0 to 100.
● Ask an adult to point to the numbers on the number line if you need help.
● Repeat the activity, but this time march in time to your counting.
● Continue marching as you count in fives, but this time clap on every ten as well. Identify what these numbers will be the first time through if necessary.
● Repeat this, but this time clap on the fives.
● Do the activity again, but this time count backwards.
● Each time you clap, it is on a number in the five times table.

NOW TRY THIS

1. Try counting in twos and clapping on every other number (the fours).
2. Try counting in threes and clapping on every other number (the sixes) and so on, to learn other times tables.

ALPHABET NAMES

THINKING SKILL: information processing
SUBJECT LINK: English (literacy)
LEARNING LINK: auditory
ORGANISATION: whole class and then groups of six
RESOURCES: whiteboard; paper; pencils

WHAT TO DO

● Ask the children to recite the alphabet, clapping each time they say a letter.
● Write down a word you want the children to learn, or one that has seven or eight letters such as *alphabet, February, rainbow, because, another, together*. It can be any word, just as long as nearly all its letters are different because the focus of the activity is a fun way to recall alphabetical order rather than being able to read the word.
● Tell the children that you are going to say the alphabet again. This time, every time you come to a letter that appears in the word they must put their hands in the air.
● Afterwards talk about how to make the activity easier.
● Put the letters of the word into alphabetical order.
● Try the activity again.
● Did the children find this easier?

NOW TRY THIS

1. Organise the children into smaller groups.
2. Ask each child to write down their first name and to put the letters in alphabetical order.
3. When they are ready, say the alphabet as a group, each child standing up every time a letter that appears in their name is said.

POSITION

THINKING SKILL: information processing, reasoning
SUBJECT LINK: PE
LEARNING LINK: auditory
ORGANISATION: whole class
RESOURCES: PE benches, mats and tables; labels with position words (over, under, through, around, above, below, across, behind, in front); an adult to hold up the labels

WHAT TO DO

● Work with a friend to find apparatus that you can stand in front of, stand behind, stand beside, stand between, be one above and one below one another, move over, under, across and around.
● Look at the word being held up by your teacher. Move to the position of the word.
● Ask your teacher to make a sequence with the words.
● With a friend, put together a sequence to mirror the words. Use only one piece of apparatus.
● Show your sequence to the class.
● Watch other children's sequences. Are they like yours?

DANCING LETTERS (1)

THINKING SKILL: information processing
SUBJECT LINK: PE
LEARNING LINK: auditory
ORGANISATION: whole class
RESOURCES: a piece of music with a steady 32 beats, such as *In Dulce Jubilo* by Mike Oldfield; chalk; a large area to dance (either in the hall or playground)

WHAT TO DO

● Draw a very large **c** on the ground.
● Look at where others have drawn a **c**. Decide which you will dance round after you have danced round yours.
● As the music plays, dance around your letter **c**, then move to another **c** and dance around that. Keep dancing around the letter **c**s until the music finishes.
● Turn your **c** into an **o**.
● Now dance around the letter **o** in the same way.
● Turn your letter **o** into an **a** by adding a descender at the side.
● Decide where you need to start.
● Learn this rhyme to dance the letter **a**: *Dance around the **c** first, join it up and down the stick.*
● Dance around the **a**s, saying the rhyme as you dance to make sure you start at the right place and dance in the right direction. You may want to put a green dot at the start and a red dot where you finish.

NOW TRY THIS

Turn some of your letters into **g**, **d**, **q** and the number **9**. Make up rhymes and dance around the letters in time to the music.

DANCING LETTERS (2)

THINKING SKILL: information processing
SUBJECT LINK: PE
LEARNING LINK: auditory
ORGANISATION: whole class
RESOURCES: a piece of music with a steady 32 beats, such as ' by Mike Oldfield; chalk; a large area to dance (either in the hall or playground)

WHAT TO DO

● Draw a very large **s** on the ground.
● Look at where others have drawn an **s** and decide which one you will dance round after

you have danced round yours.
● As the music plays, dance around your letter **s**, then move to other **s**s and dance around those until the music finishes.
● Turn your **s** into an **8**.
● Now dance around the number **8**s in the same way.
● Decide where you need to start.
● Learn this rhyme to dance the number **8**: *Dance around the **s** first, join it up to make an **8**.*
● Make sure you start at the right place and dance in the right direction. You may want to put a green dot at the start and a red dot where you finish.

NOW TRY THIS

1. Identify a letter or number you often get wrong when writing.
2. Ask an adult to help you draw this on the ground.
3. Put a green dot where to start your dance and a red dot where to finish.
4. Dance around this letter or number to the music.

UP AND DOWN SOUNDS

THINKING SKILL: reasoning
SUBJECT LINK: music
LEARNING LINK: auditory
ORGANISATION: whole class or small groups
RESOURCES: a copy of 'Row, row, row your boat' in *Flying a Round: 88 Rounds and Partner Songs* (A&C Black); xylophones and glockenspiels set up with only the notes C_B, D, E, F, G, C^7

WHAT TO DO

● Learn the song 'Row, row, row your boat', listening to how the tune goes up and down.
● Stand up and sing the song.
● Every time the tune goes down, stoop down. When it goes back up, stand up tall.
● Find a xylophone or glockenspiel. Make sure it only has the notes C_B, D, E, F, G, C^7.
● Work out the tune, recalling your movements when the tune goes up and down.
● When you have succeeded, practise the tune a few times before performing it to the class.

NOW TRY THIS

1. Choose a song you all know.
2. Sing it through. As you sing, move up and down with the tune.

DOUBLE SOUNDS

THINKING SKILL: reasoning
SUBJECT LINK: English (literacy)
LEARNING LINK: auditory
ORGANISATION: whole class
RESOURCES: board with the alphabet written on it

WHAT TO DO

● Say the letters of the alphabet, following the letters on the board as you say them.
● With a friend, identify which letters have more than one sound (**c, g, a, e, i, o, u**).
● Agree, as a class, which letters have more than one sound.
● Ask an adult to mark these with an asterisk.

NOW TRY THIS

1. This time, clap on every letter but stand up or wave your hands in the air when you get to a letter that has two or more phonemes.
2. Repeat the game, but this time stand up or wave your hands in the air when you get to a letter that can be silent such as **g, k, w** and **p**.

UP, DOWN AND ACROSS

THINKING SKILL: information processing
SUBJECT LINK: PE
LEARNING LINK: auditory
ORGANISATION: whole class, with children divided into four groups.
RESOURCES: a large space; a piece of lively music

WHAT TO DO

● Ask each group to stand in a different corner of the hall. Point out that *horizontal* is across the hall from side to side, *vertical* is across the hall from bottom to top (or top to bottom) and *diagonal* is corner to corner.
● Ask one group to move horizontally across the hall. Now ask another group to move across the hall vertically. Continue until all groups have each moved horizontally, vertically and diagonally, although this should take no more than two minutes.
● Now try this out with all groups moving together. Remind them about safety when crossing each other's paths. Start with horizontal and vertical moves only. When you think the children are ready, try diagonal.
● Put the dance to music with you calling out vertical, diagonal or horizontal to direct the groups' movement across the hall.

NOW TRY THIS

1. Give each group one minute to work out a four-part dance sequence. It is quite simple for them to do this so they should not need too much time. Alternatively, choose a leader for each group and let them make instantaneous decisions as to which way to go each time.
2. As each group demonstrates their dance, the other children should say in which direction the group is moving: vertically, horizontally or diagonally.

JUMP AROUND THE CLOCK

THINKING SKILL: information processing
SUBJECT LINK: mathematics
LEARNING LINK: auditory
ORGANISATION: whole class or groups
RESOURCES: a set of clock faces drawn on the playground outside or large space inside (the circles should be large enough for all the children to stand across to touch 12 or 9 with one foot and 6 or 3 with the other); playground chalk

WHAT TO DO

● Play a version of the game 'What's the time Mr Wolf?' An adult or a friend should ask you (the wolf) what the time is and you show them with your arms.
● For example, for one o'clock, one arm should be pointing directly upwards to 12 for o'clock and the other one pointing to where number 1 would be on the clock. Go around the clock.

NOW TRY THIS

1. Turn the circles on the floor into clocks by adding the numbers around the outside.
2. Play the game again, but this time jump your feet into position on the numbers. So, for example, for 1 o'clock you will have your left foot on the 12 and your right foot on the 1.
3. Continue the game until you have all had a turn to jump around the clock.
4. Play the game again, but this time jumble up the times so that you may be asked to jump to any time in random order.